REAL PEOPLE REAL CHANGE

STORIES OF A
CHANGE WARRIOR
IN THE
BUSINESS WORLD

Donna Strother Highfill

PIPING TREE
PUBLISHING
RICHMOND VIRGINIA

Real People, Real Change:
Stories of a Change Warrior in the Business World
Copyright © 2011 Donna Strother Highfill

ISBN 978-0-9836496-0-1

Donna S. Highfill
www.highfillperformancegroup.com
Phone 804-723-4284

The stories in this book involve real people and real change, however, certain elements such as names and business types have been modified to protect the clients' anonymity.

Cover and book design by Sherry Wachter
www.sherrywachter.com

Editorial and Production Services by Maureen R. Michelson
www.newsagepress.com

Printed in the United States

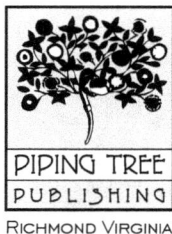

PIPING TREE
PUBLISHING
RICHMOND VIRGINIA

Dedication

To Neil Karn, whose incredible knowledge of organizational change has been a wellspring of insight, providing invaluable sustenance for this change warrior's journey.

Acknowledgments

Change succeeds because people work together. A sense of community makes the unknown less frightening, and gives people the strength to make the change journey.

I have found that writing a book is no different. Through this process, I have had the honor of working with a community of people who became both teachers and motivators.

I thank Brenda Peterson, my concept editor and friend, who inspired my heart with her gentle guidance and helped me create the canvas upon which I shared my stories. Maureen R. Michelson then took her editor's paintbrush and, with incredible attention to detail, painted a clear, concise picture. Finally, designer Sherry Wachter provided a visual identity that will appeal to the reader.

I thank my husband for sharing his organizational development brilliance, and for spending many hours listening to me struggle for the right words. I thank my mom for telling me I could do it even when I didn't believe that I could; my daughter, Samantha, for providing her writer's expertise; and my son, Jacob, for his director's eye.

Finally, I want to thank all of my clients for the honor of making the change journey with them. From each of you I have learned invaluable lessons, and I am amazed by what you are willing to sacrifice to make your organizations better.

These are the people that form my community, and I believe traveling with a community of others is the only way to change the world.

Contents

Introduction. ix

Section One: Engage the Heart

    Chapter I: Real Change Warriors 3

    Chapter II: Make a Humble Entrance 9

    Chapter III: Build Trust with a Balanced Perspective 19

    Chapter IV: Find Common Ground. 31

Section Two: Inform the Mind

    Chapter V: Conduct an Assessment. 45

    Chapter VI: Deliver the Teachable Moment 59

Section Three: Move the Feet

    Chapter VII: Value Progress Over Popularity 73

    Chapter VIII: Find Change Disciples. 83

    Chapter IX: Provide Quick and Simple Wins 93

Section Four: Light a Fire

    Chapter X: The Courage to Change 107

    Chapter XI: People Still Follow the Leader 119

Section Five: Stay Focused

    Chapter XII: Some Will Follow, Some Will Fall. . . 131

    Chapter XIII: Phasing Out Phantoms 139

Section Six: Recognize a New Reality

    Chapter XIV: From Chaos to Cooperation. 151

    Chapter XV: When to Wave Good-bye. 161

About the Author 168

Introduction

*I*f you think change is a choice, you need to think again. In this immensely competitive world where a new idea is emulated and improved upon in a matter of days, we do not have the luxury of sitting around deciding if we really want to change. Change is a part of life, and in the business world, real change is essential if you want to thrive and prosper. Hopefully, we do our best to choose the right change to make. Sometimes we do, sometimes we don't. But for those leaders who have the courage to try, who understand that change is difficult and are willing to face the harshest realities, and soldier through—they will succeed.

Great change leaders understand that unless leaders provide specific actions to help people build a bridge between knowing and actually doing, there is no change. The stories and lessons in this book are ones that I have lived and learned over the past twenty-five years. Hopefully, they will help you discover your own identity as a change warrior, along with your own techniques and processes.

Some of you are change leaders by trade, others are being asked to be temporary change warriors in your current leadership position. This book will help you through a variety of challenging situations that call for change.

You could benefit from this book if:

- You are an executive in a company who needs to make a change and get fast results.
- You are an external consultant trying to create change within a company.
- You are an internal leader who has been asked to install a new process or technology.
- You have been asked to initiate a change and people are not moving and you are not sure why
- You are a project manager who can't seem to get your project to move forward.

The truth is each one of us is asked to lead change at some point in our lives. Whatever your change assignment may be, the information and stories in this book will be helpful. This is the book I wish somebody had shared with me years ago.

So, read on! These stories and change lessons will provide you with a map of dos and don'ts that will help you avoid tripwires and find the golden compass of change. If you have picked up this book, I am guessing you are a warrior in the making. Welcome!

SECTION ONE

Engage the Heart

"Some people change when they see the light, others when they feel the heat."

Caroline Schoeder
American Writer

CHAPTER I

Real Change Warriors

My telephone rings, and it is another company that wants help with its sales culture. Amazingly, management had rolled out great training and kicked off its new sales program with lots of fanfare, but after a year, the company's sales numbers were not getting any real lift. I am not surprised when I hear this, but I know my client is. Slowly and respectfully, I explain to management that this result is not about bad training or a lazy work force, but rather this is about change and how employees resist what is not familiar.

Bottom line, change is all about heart. It isn't just about charts or data or project plans or fun acronyms. Real change has a noble goal, and must be built on well-worn paths while providing some emotional trailblazing.

Regularly, I write about change on my blog. And regularly, readers respond with comments that reflect a general cynicism about the whole prospect of change. Some of the cynical responses I have received to my stories or quotes about positive change, include:

- "I'm tired of change being shoved down my throat by leaders I don't respect. If I liked the leader, I'd do it. But I don't."

- "All change isn't good — and I think we need to think about why we're changing before we do it. That's all I'm saying."
- "Change is a topic used by hundreds of consultants to make big money, roll in with their new models and charts, and then roll out in a few years, millions of dollars richer while the company is worse off than it was before."

You know what? I agree with every one of these statements! I don't think the term "change agent" begins to reflect the energy, inspiration, and commitment it takes to lead change. That is why I call myself a "change warrior."

Since 1990, I have helped companies make remarkable transitions because I am willing to work hard and stay with the mission until it is completed. I am not a wizard that performs magic, but I am a proud change warrior who works hard for real change. And I stand by the people and leaders of companies as fellow change warriors, preparing them to stay firm when the going gets tough and celebrate when the transition is complete.

Unfortunately, the word *change* has a negative connotation due to false change leaders who believe more in building their resume than actually making a difference. They are what I call "faux change agents," and they practice a bait and switch called "faux change." Some signs of false change can include:

- Change that is used exclusively to build a resume.
- New tasks that keep people busy but don't move anything forward.
- Presentations and opinions that invalidate the past rather than building on it.
- Project plans that organize work but don't touch the behavior of those impacted.

- Change that creates a hamster wheel of meetings without noticeable improvement.
- Change that goes away before results are seen, leaving a "this too shall pass" mentality.

Experience with faux change agents creates a general cynicism that results in disbelief in the power of real change. Employees begin to see change as a ruse, or a ridiculous effort that will pass if ignored. In addition, too many companies implement frantic change efforts that are implemented in the wrong situations, for the wrong people, in the wrong way.

Most leaders forget that real change involves real people. They must remember that behind each employee are a family, a need, and a desire to make a difference in the world. If employees think their job might change, they worry about how they will support those they love. Their on-the-job stress will impact relationships at home. If someone they work with is impacted negatively, they will hurt for that individual and feel survivor's guilt if they stay on the job while that individual is fired or laid off. The process of change affects not just employees' conscious rational thoughts, but creates subconscious emotional reactions.

Real change warriors take into account employees' lives in the office as well as outside the office, and promote change that:

- Is the right thing to do.
- Builds on the strengths of the past.
- Makes the company more competitive.
- Builds the skills and spirit of the employees.
- Provides specific steps that are implementable.
- Positively changes the behavior of those impacted.
- Provides specific behaviors that provide an actionable recipe for next steps.

- Stays around until the change becomes the new comfort zone.

Real change cannot be completed quickly. It involves a journey that will include failures and victories, tears and smiles, accomplishments and regrets. The majority of a change process deals with emotions, not rational decisions. Letting go of a comfort zone creates fear. The realization that something is over provokes tears. Letting go to reach a next step creates fear, and reaching a new reality evokes cheer. The process can't be shortened or rushed, because it is a process that involves human beings.

CHANGE LESSON

Real Change Is a Challenge

True leaders of change understand that the journey will require tremendous heart and tenacity. So many executives try to order change, and fall victim to the "faux change agents" they hire who will promise anything just to get the job. Most change agents are actually project managers who believe listing tasks on a report is the same thing as getting people to change.

The confusion between faux change and real change causes a certain cynicism among business leaders that undercuts the successful and real change efforts of what I call change warriors.

CHANGE LESSON

Change Warriors Are Passionate

The term "change agent" makes it sound like the agent is representing the change itself rather than championing the people at the company who will be impacted. For me, the term "change warrior" reflects the depth of commitment you must have to a company's leaders and employees who will be involved in the change that will move the company forward. Change warriors understand that change can involve emotional battles and require intelligent, strategic planning. We understand that moving people along the path of change is the most challenging part. Change warriors also believe passionately in the change they are instituting, They know building on the company's past is critical, and they must engage people's hearts while providing a clear map of what will be required to make change happen.

CHAPTER II

Make a Humble Entrance

*I*f people want to do something, they call it an opportunity. If they don't want to do it, they call it change. That is why I tell clients, "If you want to lead change, you must be prepared to be warriors." In most organizations, leaders will be asked to make changes that require moving the hearts and minds of large groups of people, many of whom do not see the value in the new way of doing things. Until employees are clear on the value of making a particular change, leaders will only capture forward movement on paper.

Change warriors must balance the discomfort of change while simultaneously engaging the hearts of those who will be key players in the change initiative. Warriors know that creating change is usually not a gentle process, but they also know that unless they enroll the hearts of the people impacted, the change will never convert to actual behaviors. It is essential to always remember the humanity of change, otherwise your efforts will be stalled. I learned this valuable lesson on my first sales job.

On my first day as a salesperson, I wore a navy blue business suit that looked especially nice and professional. I was going to sell radio ads in the Midwest's expansive farmland peppered with small towns spread thirty or more miles apart. As the newest salesperson at a radio station with a 200,000 watt FM station and a 5,000 watt AM station, I had been given a few house accounts and a list of other accounts that nobody else could turn into anything. That is always the fun part of being the new sales hire; the other team members can get rid of their dead accounts.

Like many new salespeople, I didn't receive any formal training and headed out that hot summer morning with a paper map and the Yellow Pages. I was young, inexperienced, and therefore, ridiculously confident. I drove my pride and joy—a new, brown Datsun 310 hatchback that I had bought myself. I really loved my car but it had vinyl seats and no air conditioning, which became problematic in the 83° degree heat with almost 100% humidity. It was only a matter of time before the back of my legs would become a permanent part of the driver's seat.

As I drove to my first appointment at 8:00 a.m., my business suit was already soaking wet. At a stoplight, I peeled off my panty hose. Despite the stifling heat and my general discomfort, when I pulled into the parking space in front of the hardware store, I was ready to make a big impression on my first client.

The radio station owner had advised me to get to know my customers before attempting a sale. I didn't heed his advice because I knew that aggressive salespeople went for the "close" as quickly as possible. While I had no formal sales training, I had read several sales book that talked about how to get past the gatekeeper, get to the owner, hook their interest, and then close the deal—all in the first visit!

As soon as I walked in the front door of the hardware store, I began searching for the gatekeeper I had read about. My sense was the gatekeeper would be an administrative assistant of some kind, but all I saw was a man in overalls stocking boxes of nails on a shelf. The rest of the store looked like an old fashion general store on a movie set for Westerns, complete with tumbleweeds rolling across the dirt street outside, and devoid of human life. In my mind, I declared the man in the overalls as the gatekeeper, and confidently walked toward him.

I turned up the wattage on my salesperson smile that I had practiced in the mirror that morning. My high heels clicked on the cracked tile floor, which seemed to startle him because he dropped the box of nails. Luckily, they didn't spill. "I hope I didn't cause that!" I said as I laughed lightly, trying to make eye contact. He looked at me briefly and then averted his eyes, still busy with the nails.

As I closed in, ready to give my sales pitch, he backed away, mumbled something, and turned to walk down the aisle. For a large man, he moved quickly. I followed, saying, "Excuse me, sir? Sir?" He almost broke into a jog, headed for the Employees Only door as if it were his escape route from hell. If that door hadn't been available, I think he would have walked through a brick wall to get away from me.

I decided that maybe he wasn't the gatekeeper after all, so I clicked around the store in my professional high heels looking for this nebulous character, the gatekeeper. After ten minutes, I finally picked up a pack of gum and waited at the cash register. My sales book had emphasized that tenacity was the most important quality of successful sales people, so I was not about to leave until I met the owner of the store.

Looking through my purse for cash to pay for the gum, I caught the sight of denim in my peripheral vision. The man in overalls was back.

"May I help you?" he asked in a voice he might use with a robber pointing a gun at him.

"Yes, I'm looking for the owner of the store. Can you help me find him?" I asked with a smile so fake I must have looked like a Miss America contestant with gas pains.

"I'm the owner. What do you want?"

I was not prepared for him to be the owner. Still standing by the cash register, I decided to stick to the purchase for the time being.

"Well, I was thinking I might get some of this gum."

He rang it up, poking the keys of his old cash register like he had a personal vendetta against it.

"What are ya sellin'?" he asked, aware I was there for something else.

Oddly, I felt exposed. "Well, I work with the radio station, and I'd like to talk to you about a special we're running on some ads right now. I notice there are not a lot of customers in here this morning, and I think some morning ads are just what you need. We have a really good price on them right now, and ...."

I proceeded to pull brochures out of my folder, sure that I was getting ready to close my first deal. The owner ran his hand over his balding head, scratched his ear, and then made the first real eye contact of the day.

"Young lady, I don't know you. Now, you need to leave my store."

All the advice in my sales books raced through my mind as I tried to figure out how to handle this objection and still save the sale. I decided to go for the infamous "feel, felt, found theory."

"Well, I understand how you *feel*, many of my customers have *felt* that way, but they *found* ...." Thank goodness the storeowner interrupted me, because I had no client experience and would not have been able to finish the sentence.

"What do you know about me? Or my store? Or this town?" he demanded.

I stood there with my mouth open; sure that something brilliant would emerge. Nothing did. I simply stood there like a bass waiting for the hook.

"That's what I thought, young lady. We're done here."

And we were. I walked out with my head down and my sense of sales savvy squashed under the direct gaze of an angry man in overalls. I went back to the radio station rather than to my next sales call, ready to admit that I was an absolute failure when it came to sales. This town was small enough that the owner of the hardware store had already called Jack, the radio station manager, who met me at the front door, laughing.

"So, you met Harry, did ya?"

"I guess—is he the owner?" I asked in a ridiculously naive way.

"You didn't even know his name before you talked to him?" Jack asked in disbelief. "Do you know anything about this town and the people who have spent most of their lives here? You don't just sell an ad to somebody, especially when you're an outsider. You make sure you know their name, how long they've been in business, what's important to them. You walk in with a cup of coffee, dressed in blue jeans—not a fancy business suit. You sit down in a rocking chair at the front of their store and sip on coffee, asking them about their last fishing trip and their grandson's football game."

"And then they'll buy the ad?" I asked, still anxious for the sale.

"No!" Jack said, shaking his head. "Then they'll be ready to talk to you the next time when you stop by, unless you've already made them angry on the first visit. You think it's hard building trust in this town? Try rebuilding it."

Jack paused for a moment, and then continued the lesson. "That's what you've got to do now. But if you'd done it right the first time, then on the next visit they'll thank you for the coffee. And, if you're lucky, they'll ask you about *your* life.

"This goes on until one day, a month or so down the road, they ask about the radio station and how things are going there. *Then* you can mention the advertising we might offer them. Go in the door humble, and leave humble."

Speechless, I just listened, realizing I truly knew next to nothing on how to be a salesperson. I was still skeptical of this approach. "And what if he doesn't want to talk to me?" I had all sorts of horrible thoughts of being physically escorted out of his store.

"If you find out his favorite kind of coffee and bring it to him, or ask him about his grandkids, or bring him doughnuts, he'll talk to you eventually." I nodded slowly, wanting to absorb the confidence the manager exuded.

"Now, get back out there!" the station manager commanded. "Selling is filled with a lot more people saying 'No' than 'Yes.' Selling requires a real concern for the people and a thick skin. So get to know your customers. They're good people. Make a humble entrance. Respect their business."

I heeded Jack's advice and found that some customers didn't wait an entire month before buying, and others waited even longer. Most importantly, I learned that truly changing somebody's mind has to begin with a respect for who that person is and what he or she has done in life. I learned that people sniff each other out emotionally, making sure that we are all part of the same human pack. Clients want to connect with you before they change their mind about anything.

My radio station manager taught me that you give other people your energy first before asking them to spend the money they have worked so hard to make. You work hard to earn their business, and you start by connecting in an honest and real way—head down and heart open.

CHANGE LESSON

Build Trust

Change warriors need to build trust by showing their intent is to add value to the people impacted rather than just "sell" the change process. Enter a situation in a way that shows respect for what has been done in the past and for the people who made it happen. Caution: Change warriors do not want to be introduced by the CEO as the "next big thing" to hit the company.

If you are an independent change warrior, or what I call an "external warrior" hired to work with a company on changes, you do not want to begin by verbally providing an impressive resume. People are not moved by somebody else's success. Instead, they are influenced by those who seem to care about them. Begin your first meeting by finding out as much as you can about those you will ask to change.

(Change Lesson, cont.)

If you already work for the company, an "internal warrior," and you will be leading the change, do not assume everyone in the company knows who you are or understands your new role. You need to begin your change relationships with a clean slate, explaining your new role carefully to the change team so they can disassociate you from a current leadership position and see you with different eyes. You are now a change warrior, and their temporary leader.

As a change warrior, whether external or internal, enter that first meeting with humility and positive intent. Exchange additional facts about who you are later on with individuals over a cup of coffee. Be authentic in your caring, and be sure to stop asking about budget and inquire about family. Remember: If the company's employees resist you as a change warrior from the beginning, you will have the uphill struggle of rebuilding trust.

CHANGE LESSON

Read Your Audience

The change you are promoting does not have a chance without your ability to connect with people and lead them through a new initiative. Any change warrior who enters with the intent of defeating his or her audience has lost the relationship before it ever had a chance to exist.

Watch body language carefully as you walk through the door for an initial visit. Some people will be smiling and making eye contact, attempting to make you feel welcome. They are generally the supporters. Others will be making eye contact with a hesitant smile, maybe leaning over to someone close to them, whispering. They tend to be the ones who are more fearful, and they could already be gathering supporters for the day when they will turn on you. Others might just run through the door that says "Employees Only" and try to get away from you.

Respect your audience enough to pay attention to them. Not one process in the history of the world succeeded without a leader's ability to influence other people. Always start with humility, shift to empathy, accelerate with curiosity, and build by being consistent and trustworthy. Trust is never built in one visit, but it can be destroyed in one visit. Change doesn't occur because it is commanded; change occurs because we have connected with the heart of those who will make it happen.

CHAPTER III

Build Trust with a
Balanced Perspective

Change is too often seen as a type of project that can be put on a spreadsheet and orchestrated by a lot of consultants and appointed employees who invade your company like so many ants. They come scurrying in with a pre-packaged solution that has nothing to do with the work culture they are attempting to change. Consultants often offer solutions too quickly without first establishing a foundation of trust by getting to know the employees they are asking to change.

When my kids were young, I decided to step out of consulting and work with a high school located in the inner city in a high-crime district. I was subbing for a teacher who was going to be on maternity leave. I ended up teaching the class and working as a change warrior. The school's new principal faced change issues because the retiring principal had a very different approach to discipline and teaching. His hardline approach with the students required them to be seen and not heard. Classrooms had to be quiet. Fighting of any kind was not tolerated, and students were sent to detention on a regular basis.

Because of the rough neighborhood, I didn't fault the outgoing principal for his approach. However, the students who wanted to learn and interact in the classroom were not allowed to do much of anything except answer the teacher's questions. There was very little creativity, and even less laughter.

The new principal was desperately trying to shift the environment from one of total command and control to one where the kids could feel free to be creative and valued. When the new principal found out I was a change consultant taking a one-year break to spend time with my kids, he asked for my help.

I thought that dealing with my class, labeled the "Severely Emotionally Disturbed" (SED) class, would be the toughest thing I would do. I was wrong. As a new and inexperienced teacher, being put into the role of change warrior was the toughest part of my new job. In fact, many of the teachers perceived me as the ultimate suck-up to the principal. I was used to corporate audiences that were politically correct and polite, so I was a little startled by the teachers who actually ignored me in the hallways. Fortunately, my experience in change management had prepared me for this kind of situation.

First, I needed to assess the current situation before I attempted any kind of change. My initial judgment was that there were two categories of teachers:

1) About 25% of the teachers loved their students no matter how tough they were to teach, and and purchased classroom materials to teach more creatively.

2) The remaining 75% of the teachers looked like they couldn't get a job teaching anywhere else. They couldn't stand the students, and it seemed as if their biggest motivation was getting summers off.

Instantly, I knew the new principal was in a tough situation since I determined that 75% of his teachers barely had the energy to stay around until 2:45 when school ended, much less put energy into any kind of change effort. In addition, this school did not have teachers lining up with a desire to help the less fortunate. Instead, it was the graveyard where burnt-out teachers could end their career.

Truthfully, I had no real understanding of what it would be like to teach in this school for ten or twenty years and how exhausted and discouraged these teachers might be. At the time I made my initial assessment and judgment, I didn't know that teachers often had to forfeit their one free block of time because they had to substitute a class for another teacher who was absent. Later, I would learn there were only about three substitute teachers from the entire school district who were willing to substitute teach at this school, so the teachers at the school had to cover for one another. And beyond the teaching challenges, there were numerous details they struggled with daily. For instance, in the teachers' break room where the copier broke at least once a day, teachers often fought over one sheet of paper since they had to provide their own. I was unaware of these difficulties at the time I prepared for a change plan.

Instead, I moved too quickly, basing my decisions on assumptions, not reality. I judged the teachers' behavior as simply a lack of enthusiasm. Determined to make a change, I decided I would institute the classic change process I had used in corporations. I told the new principal, "Most people only change because there is either tremendous benefit in the change or tremendous pain if the change is not made. We need to find something that will propel them forward."

In our planning meeting, the principal and I decided an aggressive change session was necessary and I would be the one to lead it. We imagined this change session would kick off the new school year and successfully propel teachers down a new path.

Plans that fail are usually plans that ignore the heart. The change session failed, not because the teachers were stubborn, but because their change warrior (me) started down the change path without first learning about their situation. My presentation, while upbeat, basically accused the teachers of being unwilling to change. I failed to respect their situation.

At one point, I said, "Change requires energy and determination." One of the gray-haired teachers raised his hand and responded, "I tried to change this place for ten years. It didn't work, and now I just want to retire." I didn't take into account that some of those teachers had been good teachers once, but were weakened by the pummeling of a broken system and the lack of forward movement.

I had arrived at the school in a bubble, descending upon these teachers who had spent years in a very tough environment, and tried to instantly engage them by telling them what to do. I expected everybody to be "wowed" by my change knowledge; instead, I found myself stumbling through the session as tired teachers stared me down. They were underpaid and worn out from battling kids and parents. In my little consulting palace, I had been making more in a day than some of them made in a month, and therefore, my lovely little change-isms didn't stick. I realized in the middle of the session what was going on, and I felt embarrassed. You have no idea how badly I wanted to say,

"You know what? This is the wrong time for me to do this. I'm sorry. Let's reconvene at the end of the year."

During my informal assessment, I found out that most of the teachers had a betting pool going as to how long I would even last as a substitute teacher with the SED students. For ten years, the classroom had been a revolving door for teachers who couldn't control the kids, so why would a 5' 3" female who had been in the lap of luxury in corporate America be able to?

Once the change session ended, I realized my informal assessment was over. I had lost the trust of the teachers, and my change-warrior license had been temporarily revoked. It was time to prove my commitment to my job as a teacher.

I spent the next few days assessing the group of kids who filled my small, stuffy classroom. Most of the students were fidgety boys, aged twelve to sixteen, who were hyperactive and from tough family situations. Many of the students lived in motels or were in foster care. Most looked at me with lost, angry gazes. The teacher taking maternity leave showed me her teaching plan, which consisted of a stack of third-grade worksheets that she handed out at the beginning of each block and a cabinet filled with old board games the students were allowed to play once they finished the worksheets.

I couldn't believe it. These worksheets took about fifteen minutes to complete, and were ridiculously simple. Just because SED students were constantly fighting didn't mean they had learning disabilities. However, because our students were prone to fighting in other classes, they did stay in their SED classes for almost five hours a day. This provided a lot of game time.

On the first day, we spent what seemed like hours playing the game of "Life," which was missing most of the parts that made the game work (like the wheel you were supposed to spin) and a board that looked like it had been chewed up by a guinea pig. A few minutes into the game a fight broke out between two of the boys and I had to break it up. By the time we were done with "Life," I understood their tension and frustration in a whole new way—I kind of wanted to fight somebody myself!

On my second day, a co-teacher, Mr. Michaels, joined me since this particular class was notoriously unruly. Fortunately for me, Mr. Michaels had a son who had many of the same behavioral issues as the boys in our class, so he was prepared. A tall, lanky man with a quick sense of humor, Mr. Michaels felt the same way I did about the current environment, and was ready to create some discomfort with the school administration in the name of improvement. Mr. Michaels was entering the teaching profession midlife and had a passion for creating a better place for kids to learn.

We spent our first free study block together preparing our plan for change. Here is what we came up with for turning this group of students around:

- Burn the third grade worksheets. Instead, develop folders for each student that provided work appropriate for his or her grade level, and a sufficient amount of work for the entire study block.
- Create a "celebration" board where everybody could show the good grades they received and, if earned, could put up papers or artwork.
- Allow journal time after every lunch period (our biggest fight club hour). Let the students write whatever they wanted as long as they wrote for twenty minutes. We would not read their journals

unless they wanted us to. These kids had a lot of anger, and we wanted them to have a chance to express it.
- Create a news team that would report on events at the school. The student reporters would work on stories for a month, and then we would film two of the students as they delivered the news. Once completed, we would send video copies to our principal and the superintendent of schools.
- Change the school's perception of these students by showing they could add value and behave well.

My co-teacher and I started our engines quickly because we knew we would need the momentum, and students needed to know things were going to be different. I would love to tell you our changes were widely accepted by all and we went on to make a movie like "Stand and Deliver," but it wasn't that easy. The students had grown used to their boring, contentious environment.

Mr. Michaels and I were regularly greeted with a lot of rolling eyes and profanity from the students, but we didn't stop. We moved forward by creating our own little tornado of activity. Each student received a colorful journal that we purchased ourselves. Then we gave them thirty minutes a day to write anything they wanted—even if they just repeated the same curse word, which several did.

Our intent was to get the students calmed down after lunch, and to let them know that somewhere in the world they were given privacy and treated with respect. Our hope was to encourage a sense of responsibility for using the gift they were given. In addition, these were kids who got very few gifts and even fewer breaks in life.

Our next step was to take the writing skills developed during our journal time and get the students to start writing stories about their school. In addition, we had our SED students interview other teachers so they could begin to build positive relationships with these teachers. The goal was to mainstream the SED students into regular classes, but unfortunately, most teachers would do anything to keep SED students out of their classrooms because of the inevitable fights. We also had our students talk to other students about their lives so they could realize they weren't alone in their situations. At the end of the month, Mr. Michaels and I chose two students to present their stories in front of the camera for taping a news show.

After the first month of big change in the SED classroom, our lead anchor for the first news show was a young man named Brandon, who had a high intellect and a heart of gold. When I told him we would send the superintendent a copy of the newscast, Brandon shook like a Chihuahua in winter. We practiced his presentation for a couple of weeks in front of the camera, and he took a lot of teasing from our classroom bully, who clearly resented the attention Brandon was getting. The class bully tried to scare Brandon away from the presentation by telling him that he would "beat his ass" if he actually did the newscast. Brandon didn't scare easily; he lived in financial poverty with a sister who had cerebral palsy. He had fought for her all of his life.

The day of the video shoot Brandon walked into the classroom in his best Sunday clothes. We hadn't mentioned what he was to wear, since we knew most of these kids had very few clothes. When he walked in with his red dress shirt and blue blazer I almost cried. When I said, "Brandon, you are so handsome," his smile lit up the room. He was terrified, but determined to make this happen.

Brandon and the other presenter came across wooden and Al Gore-ish during the shooting, but they got through it. That was what really mattered. We sent the tape to the Superintendent of Schools who wrote an article about it in the monthly newsletter that went out to principals in the school district. Our principal presented our entire class with an award. We had never seen such exhilaration and pride on the students' faces.

We did not get to ride the crest of a quick win for too long, since some of the teachers started complaining more about our students and said we were being too easy on them. In addition to our SED class, there was another SED class that had a formidable teacher who ruled with an iron fist. He did not allow any talking in his classroom and put any student who happened to mutter a word immediately into detention. A large, tall man, this teacher was a bully and he encouraged his students to bully the students in our class. This teacher looked for reasons to get our students kicked out of school, even encouraging a fight in the hall that resulted in one of our news writers being sent to the boys state school due to his previous record. This SED teacher watched passively as one student heckled one of our more volatile students. I tried to step in, but since I was overwhelmed physically by the size of the students, I asked for this teacher's help. He just smiled, shook his head in a "no" motion, and ducked back into his classroom.

Despite the wrath of a few teachers, the success of our efforts started to impress other teachers who didn't believe we could make a difference with the SED students. In time, even some of the most hard-edged teachers begrudgingly gave us respect for the positive changes we had created. Mr. Michaels and I were so proud of our "hopeless" kids who had made changes and grown far beyond anyone's expectations.

As a result of my work with the SED students, the principal let me lead a second change session at the end of the school year. This time, the teachers seemed to listen. Some even apologized for being so difficult during the year.

I learned a valuable lesson from this school experience. Change warriors have to take the time to truly understand their environment before they will be followed. And once again, I learned that a humble entrance is the way to build trust, and that rebuilding trust is a lot more difficult than doing it right in the first place.

Change warriors must understand the absolute importance of gaining the trust of those impacted by working to both assess and understand their perspective and environment. If those affected by change do not trust that your intent is sincere, they will not make the journey with you. You will head down that yellow brick road by yourself, with lots of pretty project plans and activities, but nobody with whom you can link arms and lead behavioral change. A humble entrance filled with quiet observation is the way to build trust.

CHANGE LESSON

Understand the Emotions

Experienced change warriors understand that assessing the heart's condition in the very beginning of change is critical to every change initiative. Often, a company leader has given you his or her perception of what is happening within the company. A change warrior who takes only the perception of the leader is going to be in trouble. One person's perception, even if it is the CEO's, never gives you a true feel for the entire situation.

If your informal "heart" assessment is off base, then your formal assessment will be built on a faulty foundation. One person's bias could taint the effectiveness of an entire assessment. If you want to suck-up to the leader who brought you in, feel free to follow this road. If you truly want to help this company create the change it needs, then pay attention to a variety of perspectives so you can make changes that will stick.

CHANGE LESSON

Create Trust

Trust is the foundation upon which all relationships are built. Leadership without trust is a dictatorship. If you want to make a difference, you have to earn the trust of those who will be following you. I remember talking to a group of young Marines who had just completed boot camp. They were on a plane flying home for a week, and their enthusiasm was incredible. The Marine next to me talked about his drill sergeant who made them dig a ditch in the rain on their last night. Then they had to sleep in the ditch.

"Wow," I said, "You must have really hated him for making you do that."

"Oh, no ma'am," the Marine replied. "He dug that ditch and slept in it with us. He's our leader."

Change warriors know they must prove their willingness to do the tough work before people will follow them. We must show a desire to get in the trenches and get dirty before people will believe we are anything more than leaders commanding behavior change rather than leading it. Starting with great ideas and commanding change doesn't work. Instead, change warriors must be willing to acknowledge the heartbeat behind the change, and let everyone involved know they are willing to make the journey with everybody else.

CHAPTER IV

Find Common Ground

"What's the purpose of being here?"

That was the question that kicked-off a challenging session I was co-facilitating. My journey as a change warrior had landed in a place that would teach me a very important lesson. Change tends to create polarity; most people will either support the change or fight it. Those who are undecided will tend to follow the strongest side, initially. This creates a lineup like the one found in the game "Red Rover," with each side calling for the other to "come on over," but little forward movement on the change initiative. With this kind of initial dynamic, a change warrior must quickly understand how to build bridges between the two sides so people can have a way to meet in the middle.

With this particular client, we were meeting at a beautiful resort where the conference room overlooked a beautiful golf course. We all sat around an elegant walnut table, sharing coffee and bagels. Everything was in place to make this a lovely experience. There was just one problem—we had two teams facing each other that wanted to do anything but work together. My co-facilitator, Neil, and I had to help them find common ground.

It was like a corporate high noon with two technology teams glaring at each other, hands on guns, ready to draw. Two companies had merged in that urban legend known as a "merger of equals." Everybody was waiting for the proverbial shoe to drop on one of the technology teams, but this time there didn't seem to be a clear winner. Both companies agreed that they needed everybody on board, but they also knew there were two key issues they had to resolve: a generational difference, and a workplace culture difference

Prior to the session, Neil and I had interviewed every participant so we understood the strengths of each team as well as the key issues. We wanted to know their individual stories to determine if there was any way we could merge them into one story that would work for both sides. While one gentleman pled the Fifth and refused to answer any question lest he incriminate himself, ultimately, we found out a lot about both teams through these conversations.

Team One (our nickname: Old Guard) included members who were baby boomers in their late forties and early fifties, who had been with the same company for at least twenty years. Most of them had gotten their degrees through the educational assistance offered by their company and they were extremely loyal. They were proud of their ability to achieve on a frugal budget, and tended to be more conservative in the risks they were ready to take. They had built a successful technology group in a medium-sized company. The company had been their family for twenty years, and their passion was sincere. The Old Guard was homemade, and proud of it.

Team Two (our nickname: New Hires) included members who were Generation X, in their mid-twenties and early thirties, and they liked to leap out of the box with their ideas. They had sophisticated models and brought project management discipline to the table. They had grand plans that called for a project manager's office, and most of them had been recruited nationwide. The New Hires had not been together for more than three years, but their team was also very successful.

Both teams were sure the other flew on a broomstick and wore a black hat. They were suspect of everything the other team did; certain their only intent was to incrementally annihilate the other team. The New Hires' modus operandi struck The Old Guard as wasted money and runaway elegance. The Old Guard did not understand the need to develop new areas, such as the office of project management, and they did not appreciate the fact that The New Hires had recently worked for other competitors. They were fiercely loyal and didn't trust anyone who jumped from one company to another. There was a distinct distrust for The New Hires' fascination with technology that they felt would be expensive and add nothing to the team. The Old Guard saw The New Hires as form over substance, and didn't want to go bankrupt on ideas that might or might not work.

On the other hand, The New Hires saw The Old Guard as complacent, tired, and out of touch. They could not imagine what they had learned staying in the same job for twenty years, and saw them as simply looking for a comfort zone where they could sit until retirement. They did not feel The Old Guard had a willingness to learn or stay on the cutting edge of new technology. The New Hires did not want to be pulled into an outdated world that would make them complacent and less competitive.

The financial elephant in the middle of the room was salary discrepancies. The New Hires had been hired at market value salaries, which were considerably higher than The Old Guard salaries. The salaries weren't even close, and there had yet to be any discussion about how to make the pay equitable. The Old Guard resented the difference, and The New Hires were terrified that their pay would be cut in the salary shakeout. Both sides were searching for every possible reason to get rid of the other team. And they were both terrified that they would be the one to go.

Neil and I knew this was either going to be the most successful change session we had ever conducted or it was going to be a train wreck. We realized that whenever this much fear was in one room there was always the chance that a few words rubbed together the wrong way could spark a conflagration that might destroy the session before we really got started. But we also knew we couldn't conduct a real change session by avoiding the real topics.

We started the first meeting by establishing ground rules for interaction that everyone had to commit to, such as respecting one another's opinions, listening openly, and staying solution oriented. The purpose of ground rules in change sessions is to provide a touchstone, a place to hold onto when emotions created tense interactions. The toughest ground rule with this group was asking them not to listen for the fatal flaw, but instead, to listen for things with which they could agree.

Fear does not allow for fair listening—fear is about fight or flight, neither of which involves balanced communication. I must admit my own fight or flight instincts were kicking in just standing in front of that group during the first meeting!

We faced a roomful of men who refused to look at us or at each other. There was total silence—not even the clicking of blackberry keys. My instinct was to simply say "wrong room" and get out of Dodge as quickly as possible.

Neil and I knew we would have to go for broke from the beginning in order to release the tension in the room. We began by dividing the men into their own teams to answer two questions:

- How would we describe ourselves to the other team? What have been our past successes?
- If the others had to write a description of our team, what would they say about us?

These questions allowed each team to first define itself, and then the team members could put their own fears on the table concerning how they thought the other team perceived them. Many other internal consultants at the company had warned us about this approach, saying, "You're going to make people uncomfortable from the beginning and it's going to turn into a gripe session."

Neil and I decided to trust the inherent fairness of people, and felt this was a great way to allow team members to display their side of the story and their fears at the same time. We also knew this was a way to avoid a fight because each team would state its own potential weaknesses along with its successes. That way, the members of the adversarial team would not have to provide their perceptions of the other team.

For this first part, the two teams went to separate rooms, physically moving apart as if they were Ali and Frazier. After about fifteen minutes of discussion, we brought the groups back together. The Old Guard members started by defining themselves. The leader stood, only making eye contact with his team, his voice shaking. He was pumped with adrenaline, fear, and a real desire to knock around The New Hires. He read his team's definition of itself in a booming voice as if he were an evangelist convincing a crowd to come to the altar.

Next, the leader for The Old Guard presented how they thought the younger team perceived them, and this time he made eye contact with everyone in the room. As he read their flipchart points, his voice lowered a level and grew soft. He grimaced as he read off their list, which included words like *irrelevant, cheap, no vision,* and *obsolete.* It was amazing to watch the surprise in The New Hires' eyes as they realized The Old Guard nailed some of the phrases The New Hires used to describe the other team.

At the point The Old Guard leader said *obsolete,* The New Hires jumped in, letting the older team know that they actually *valued* their experience and wanted to learn from them. Neil and I could tell from The New Hires' body language and the inflection in their voices that they were sincere. Suddenly, The New Hires were defending the Old Guard! My co-facilitator and I made eye contact, recognizing we had removed one brick out of their wall of resistance.

Next, The New Hires presented their self-definition. Their leader made eye contact with everyone in the room, reflecting the lessened tension. Strutting around the flipchart area with the confidence of a young buck, their leader read his team's definition with the same level of pride, plus a hint of curiosity in his voice. The New Hires' team definition included some of the same words The Old Guard members used to describe themselves — *loyal*, *committed*, *detailed*, and *effective*. Everyone smiled when we realized how similar the two teams' self-definitions were.

Next, the leader of The New Hires presented how they thought the older team perceived them. They used words like *greedy, resume builders, overpaid, no work ethic,* and *irresponsible young whippersnappers.* The Old Guard laughed out loud, recognizing some of their hallway conversations. Again, we were pleased when The Old Guard "'fessed up" to making some of those comments, but defended The New Hires when they used words like *irresponsible.* In addition, The Old Guard admitted they had never used some of the programs or positions The New Hires wanted to use, but that didn't mean that they weren't good ideas. Members of The Old Guard said they just didn't know enough to make a decision yet.

Once we had the teams interacting, defending each other, and understanding a little more about each other's perspective, we knew it was time to get them thinking as a single team. We asked the two teams to separate again and answer one more question:

- What are your dreams for this unified team?

The two teams went to their respective rooms, reluctantly this time, and went back to the flipcharts. They came up with a list of ten-to-twenty things they hoped the company team would accomplish.

When we reconvened in the main room, each team put its flipcharts up on the wall. We reviewed the hopes of each team and highlighted those that were the same for both. Guess what? Over 80% of the ideas and aspirations on the flipcharts were highlighted. Two very different teams had almost identical goals for the company team. This included fair salaries for everyone involved, willingness for The Old Guard to entertain new ideas, and a commitment by The New Hires to learn from the discoveries of the past.

The second morning of the two-day session, Neil and I walked into a roomful of team members talking golf, laughing, and eating breakfast. They were interacting with each other — an Old Guard sitting beside a New Hire — everyone excited about the future. Neil and I wrapped up the session and received a standing ovation and an incredible sense of energy. We knew this company team was on its way to being stronger than either team was separately. I could sense a linking of arms and a desire to take an exciting journey together.

Once the company's employees returned to the workplace, they began to put some of the strategies developed at the change session into action. Salaries were adjusted and made comparable, The Old Guard was brought up to speed on the new technology, and The New Hires learned what had worked in the past, what hadn't, and why. They still had their moments of discontent and fear, but they held onto their commitment to each other made in our change session. In time, Neil and I worked with all the employees at the company and facilitated similar change sessions.

Watching those two teams truly merge taught me that most people wake up in the morning wanting to do great work. Very few people actually say, "Today, I'd like to fight my teammates and get as little productive work done as possible." Most people take pride in their work and they want to contribute to the company's growth. We all just want to be acknowledged and heard.

Finding common ground means we cannot alienate one team without somehow damaging the other. To move adversarial groups within a company forward, you must help them find common ground so a journey can be established. As change warriors, it is our job to help employees identify and agree upon one common goal, and then create a new road to get there.

CHANGE LESSON

Learn from the Past

If there is one mistake I see people make in organizations when driving change, it is the habit of invalidating the past. Companies that have been successful in the past were successful for a reason, and that reason is the hard work of the people who built the company. Too many new change agents walk in with a "toolkit of solutions," ironically borrowed from something *they* learned in the past. Immediately, these change agents eradicate anything the current staff has done to achieve success. This concept of "I'm here to fix you" alienates every heart in the room that has sacrificed time, family, and their future to make some of these past projects happen.

In any change environment, change warriors know they must acknowledge the people who have built the company, and their efforts and passion for creating those earlier successes. It is important to keep what still works. I have observed many new leaders who spend years recreating something that, once created, looks very similar to what was already in existence. Learning from the past will save a tremendous amount of time, allowing The New Hires to focus on new, necessary ideas. It will also represent loyalty to past work, which is important to The Old Guard.

If a change warrior listens to the past, people will show him or her respect in return. More importantly, employees will value the change because they have become a part of making that change happen.

Change Lesson

Lessen the Fear and Create New Ideas

Change can be built on great ideas from the past, but it also must include creative, timely ideas to move people forward. To create the fertile ground for new ideas, people must first feel secure. People who face a threat will be so focused on survival they can only see every new idea as one more nail in his or her professional coffin. In particular, think about people who are asked to adopt new technology when they have yet to turn on a computer.

Fear is legitimate, and should never be discounted or ignored. Too many leaders push people through change without ever acknowledging the silence in the room, the increased sweating, and the fearful glances across the table. Change warriors must put the greatest fear on the table and address it. They must start a session with a question like, "How do you think the other team perceives us?" This approach lessens the quiet whispers in hallways that grow into fearful exclamations in the rumor mills. I have never seen a fear directly addressed that didn't seem smaller once people were allowed to voice it and discuss it.

Fear is energy, and once you address fear, it converts into fertile ground, prepared to receive new ideas.

SECTION TWO

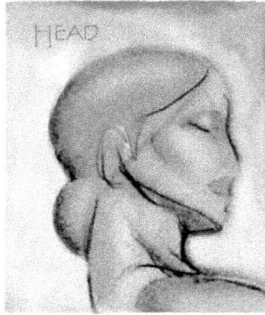

Inform the Mind

"Great changes can best be brought about under old forms."

Henry George
American Writer and Political Economist

CHAPTER V

Conduct an Assessment

A company CEO once told me, "The higher up I go, the less truth I hear." He is right, and most of the perceived *truth* that company leaders deliver comes in the form of data and statistics. While information is a small part of change, it has been the main diet of executive leadership for years. A change warrior knows that to satisfy leadership they must find ways to blend the engagement of the heart with information that will satisfy the mind. Believe me, as a change warrior you do not want to meet with CEOs or other high level executives without having supportive data. Data is what they know, it is what they are most comfortable with, and it should be a part of any change presentation. A presentation that speaks only to the heart fails to appeal to reason, and since data speaks only to the mind, there is a calming detachment that gives the listener time to think clearly.

My journey as a change warrior has revealed that an assessment done with open-ended questions generally gives me the information I need to understand the environment. Generally, I don't trust paper surveys with multiple choice questions because I believe the questions are written in a way that can lead respondents. Often, the person who created the assessment is fishing for certain answers rather than the truth.

In addition, paper (or online) assessments don't capture body language, intonation, and emotion.

So, when I do an assessment, I talk to people in person and observe them in their work culture. My assessments rarely take more than two to four weeks to complete, and my reports are neither complex nor revealed in large PowerPoint presentations. They are based on conversations with employees in the company who will be impacted by the change.

What every change warrior needs to understand is that once a leader asks you to help with change, he or she is already behind the eight ball. In all likelihood, the company has needed this change for at least a year, and the leader has done everything in his or her power to avoid it because change is uncomfortable. So, don't expect any leader to be excited when you ask for extra time to actually get to know the environment in which you are going to be working. The company leaders really want you to say, "I know what you want, I can deliver it in the next two weeks, and then you can go back to business as usual."

One particular client requested that I help lead a significant change intervention concerning their sales process. I asked to speak to a sample of people at all levels in the company before beginning the process. The CEO's eyes grew wide with disbelief and he looked at me as if I was an alien. Certain that he had not heard me correctly, I restated my request: "Before I bring this intervention to your company, I'd like to interview people in your company from the executive to the most basic service level. I need to know how they feel and incorporate their thoughts into the final product."

Well, he looked at me as if I had said, "I'd like you to drink this cup of poison and die a slow, painful death."

The CEO responded, "Well, you can, but I thought this was just some sales training that will get the numbers up quickly."

I proceeded to explain, "Changing behavior rarely happens because of training alone, and I must first engage the hearts and heads of the recipients."

I told him an assessment would let me know what are the key resistors for the sales force as well as points of easy inspiration. I reassured him, "The interviews will let the employees know that they're part of the solution, and therefore, they'll feel more responsible for its success."

When I was done explaining how I worked, I could tell the CEO was frustrated. In that moment, I knew the change was probably needed a year ago and he had shareholders breathing down his neck. To the CEO's credit, however, he did connect me with the head of sales, Robert, who ended up being a great ally.

When I told Robert I wanted to interview employees, he threw back his head, laughed, and said, "Thank God somebody wants to hear what employees have to say! I'll do whatever you need." He shook my hand vigorously, and we knew we were new best friends.

In order to avoid resistance, the first thing Robert and I wanted to do was be absolutely clear with the employees about why I was interviewing people. Some company leaders fail to recognize that if employees don't like change, it won't stick. From past experiences with sales professionals, Robert and I knew the employees had to understand the *why* before they would even be willing to do the *what*. We also knew they would only trust the change message coming from their company leaders, not from an outside consultant.

So, Robert and I got all the leaders together and presented the sales culture plans with a head/heart/feet approach. We were absolutely clear about what was being done (head), why it was being done (heart), and what actions would have to take place to make it successful (feet).

The leaders understood that they were the ones who needed to deliver the message to the employees, and they needed to be clear as to why the company would be making changes. The leaders also understood they needed to reassure the employees of their support while going through the needed changes.

In addition, Robert and I needed to make sure all the leaders were on the same page with the message they delivered. We didn't want to have one reluctant leader saying that this assessment was being done "because corporate feels it needs to be done," while another leader, who was supportive, was saying "this assessment is being conducted to create a sales and service culture that will make us more competitive." People trust consistency of message, so we provided recommended bullet points that included language explaining the benefits. We wanted to be sure all the leaders gave the same message: Everyone would benefit from the new sales culture.

On a previous consulting job, I had learned the importance of making sure all the leaders were in sync with the same message. During a meeting on company change and an upcoming assessment, one leader immediately pulled out his Blackberry and instantly informed his employees of the upcoming interviews I would conduct. Before I even left the room after that initial meeting, the leader sent a message that said, "New consultant. Each of you will be interviewed in the next few weeks about sales. Give good answers." Weeks later, we found out about this email when all of his sales employees gave the same kinds of answers to open-ended questions.

Change warriors know messages about company changes must be delivered face-to-face. Never deliver change messages via emails or memos. Any message delivered in that format screams lack of leader support and respect. I don't care if the leader is in the hospital—she or he should get on Skype and show his or her face to the employees.

Change warriors also understand that leaders need to have a balanced approach in their delivery, avoiding the temptation to oversell the change as something amazingly wonderful. People don't trust cotton-candy speeches anymore—even from leaders at the highest level in the company. How many times have employees heard the corporate-approved rah-rah speech of "this is great news for everybody," only to later find out the company is downsizing and those who remain will work extra hours? Employees would rather know that things might be tough but there is a payoff at the end of the road.

Robert and I made sure the message was honest and leaders were prepared to deliver the message in a way that built realistic enthusiasm. We used the Stockdale Paradox as our foundation. Admiral James Bond Stockdale was one of the most highly decorated officers in the history of the United States Navy. He was also a prisoner of war in Vietnam, where he survived routine beatings and torture. He created the Stockdale Paradox, which is based on a conversation with business author and well-known corporate consultant, Jim Collins, who wrote about Stockdale's Paradox in his book, *Good to Great*. Collins asked Stockdale about his time as a prisoner of war (POW) and specifically, "Who didn't make it out?"

"Oh, that's easy," Stockdale replied "The optimists."

"The optimists? I don't understand," Collins responded, now completely confused, given what Stockdale had said earlier about his POW experience.

"The optimists," repeated Stockdale. "Oh, they were the ones who said, 'We're going to be out by Christmas.' And Christmas would come, and Christmas would go. Then they'd say, 'We're going to be out by Easter.' And Easter would come, and Easter would go. And then Thanksgiving, and then it would be Christmas again. And they died of a broken heart."

Stockdale observed it was the soldiers who followed a specific discipline who survived their experience in the POW camps. "This is a very important lesson," explained Stockdale. "You must never confuse faith that you will prevail in the end — which you can never afford to lose – with the discipline to confront the most brutal facts of your current reality, whatever they might be."

Although our situation with driving change at a company was nowhere near as challenging as Stockdale's experiences as a POW, we were inspired. For our plan to make company changes, Robert and I believed our change would prevail in the end. We accepted the fact that while the process wouldn't be anything like Stockdale's experience, his paradox would still be relevant.

Once we had met with leadership and given them a deadline for presenting the assessment message, the company's sales leader worked with me to set up scheduled interviews. We sent people the questions ahead of time so they wouldn't be concerned about what was coming. Some people worry this approach results in employee preparation that will hide the truth. However, a good interviewer can see through false answers by watching an interviewee's body language and paying attention to the inconsistency of answer styles.

In addition, we also let interviewees know that our final report would not use names and locations. Our intent was to understand what employees needed in order to achieve a true sales culture. We also reassured interviewees; there were no right or wrong answers, we simply needed the truth.

Boy, did we get the truth. We started interviews at the CEO level. The top 10% of the company employees believed they had a strong sales and service culture that was competitive but could be improved. Management had invested in a multi-million dollar sales and service training program two years earlier, and had seen some lift in the first year. The reason they needed help now was the lift had disappeared and their sales numbers were at an all-time low. They believed another training program would give them the spike they needed to get the annual numbers needed to keep everybody happy.

The more I interviewed middle management and the frontline of the sales force, the clearer it became there was a gap the size of the Grand Canyon between what executive management perceived as the truth of sales and what was actually true. I considered hiring some mules to give us a ride along that dangerous path we would be treading when I delivered this message to leadership!

According to the frontline, they understood how to sell; they just were not encouraged to do it. Their performance appraisals were based upon operational skills. Middle-management leaders had grown up in an operational environment and saw sales as something to be used only when executive leadership hammered them. The company's monthly monetary incentives were paid out based upon implementation of the operational process, not based on sales figures. Top management did not pay incentives for sales behaviors, and did not include sales behaviors as a part of coaching interactions.

When I realized this dynamic was going on, it was clear this company did not need a sales and service refresher—it needed CPR! I had to go back to basics, and teach sales leadership how to lead the sales process consistently and effectively.

The power of thorough assessments is finding the truth. A change warrior does not spend months trying to fix something that doesn't need to be fixed. In this situation, if I had not conducted the assessment, I would have spent months writing and delivering the sales training simply as a refresher, and missed instigating the bigger change that was needed.

Behavioral assessment is underutilized when company leaders present a change warrior with time limitations because shareholder frustration hovers over a company's performance levels. In this kind of pressurized situation, a change agent is tempted to only interview top leadership and get rolling. But change warriors know that this approach will set up their change efforts for failure. You must gather the company's cultural factors and use that knowledge to accurately predict behavioral patterns that can lead the way to change. If you don't do this, you simply have a mirror that tells a few key leaders, "You're the fairest of them all."

When I was a young internal consultant at a mid-size company, I was asked to save a product team that had been stalled on a product rollout for almost a year. The two executive leaders overseeing the product team told me they were *sure* the problem was a lack of project planning and organization on the part of the employee team they had put together to drive the project. They were losing thousands of dollars a day and wanted a quick fix. I was prepared to find the problem with the team and report back.

After my meeting with the two executive leaders, I strutted into the first employee team meeting with the confidence of Detective Colombo, ready to find the weak individuals who were pulling this noble project down. After a few minutes, I realized the anxious glances from employees at the table meant my two executive leaders had failed to tell them who I was or why I was there. Unsure what the employees were supposed to know, I simply said, "By the way, I'm here to help you all get this initiative moving forward. My name is Donna, and I'm simply looking for ways to accelerate this project." I found it curious that people sighed, smiled, and practically handed over their files when I provided that information. No defensiveness, no excuses, just pure relief.

The meeting lasted hours, and the team took extra time to share information from the past year or so. I filled an entire notebook with information, nodded my head, and said, "Mmm, hmmm," a lot, looking knowledgeable. Clearly, what the employees reported as the problem contradicted what the executive leaders reported. I was supposed to report back to the two leaders, but had no idea what I was going to tell them. I stalled for a week, hoping to have some epiphany and deliver some profound revelations to the two leaders.

Unfortunately, the second employee meeting was much like the first. I listened quietly, and realized these were very smart people who desperately wanted to do a good job. Management had not given them a clear roadmap. Instead, they were being asked to trail blaze a new path with two leaders who had two different sets of plans and very few resources.

I decided to talk to each team member separately to see what his or her perspective was. This became my first informal assessment. Those conversations saved me (and the team) another year of total chaos. What I discovered was that the two executive leaders were battling to control this particular product and neither one was willing to let go of his approach. Each of them refused to approve any action that seemed to concede a key advantage, even if it was best for the project. The problem wasn't a lack of organization, but rather the egos of the two leaders.

I had to deliver some unexpected news to the two executive leaders. They wanted a fast solution, and I needed to let them know that *they* were the problem. Reluctantly, I set up a meeting, and sat down with them. I started by saying, "I want you all to listen very closely to what I have to say, and I need you to listen with an open mind."

They sat back, folded their arms, and said, "Absolutely." I had a hard time believing they were open minded and willing to hear my assessment, especially when they folded their arms and sat back with a slamming motion.

"This team is filled with very committed people who have put years into this project and extra hours you don't even know about. But they have two plans, and two leaders, and two sets of priorities. You all are battling each other, and they're simply caught in the middle."

I proceeded to give them examples, and while the arms folded a little tighter, they did start to admit their own competitive natures. They knew I was telling them the truth, which is the key responsibility of anybody leading change. Avoid political games, because if you play them, then you have just stepped out of the change warrior role. Sometimes, true change warriors have to be the first to take the hits by delivering the truth.

Can you imagine if I had taken only the two leaders' perspectives and tried to fix that product rollout team? I would have addressed the wrong problem. I would have asked for new team members whom we didn't need, and we would have lost more time. Instead, the two executive leaders reached a compromise and we had the product successfully on track within six weeks. In fact, it ended up being one of the most successful product rollouts at this company.

This experience taught me a couple of important lessons as a change warrior: Change requires a clear understanding of more than one perspective; the higher up a leader moves, the less truth she or he knows. And assessments do not have to be complicated efforts with lots of charts and data. Simply, assessments can be about having the right conversations with the right mix of people.

The most important thing I learned is the key to change is rarely obvious, but it is usually simple. You know what they say about simplicity: It is so much harder to get to than you might think. Going for the pearl of wisdom requires finding the right ocean, the right spot within that vast ocean, the right oyster, and the willingness to dig through some slimy stuff to find that small point of beauty. That is what a good change warrior must be willing to do with a behavioral assessment.

CHANGE LESSON

Communicate with Everyone

While leaders are usually the ones who hire change warriors, they often do not have as clear a picture of the truth as they need to make the right decisions. What they know is what is presented to them in weekly meetings, and typically, employees do not want to tell a CEO or executive leader that things are not going as planned. Most employees spend hours spinning information in a way that will sound pleasing to an exhausted leader.

A change warrior knows that to have a clear picture of a company's challenges, he or she has to listen to the leaders and to those they lead. In the Marine Corps, this is known as "ground truth." That is, understanding both what the strategic leadership plans are and then the reality of how they are being deployed on the ground. If there are gaps between these two levels of truth, then change is not going to happen in a cohesive way. A command can be barked, but if the frontline doesn't have what it needs to carry the plan forward, the greatest strategy in the world will fall flat. Without the ground truth, the ultimate result of the intervention will be a lot of money spent with few results to show for it.

CHANGE LESSON

Dig for the Simple Solution

Assessments do not have to be complicated, but they do have to be thorough. The victory comes when patterns are noted in conversation that reveal missing pieces of the puzzle. I am always amazed at change professionals who post three hundred pages of conversational responses to their fifty questions and then create five years' worth of work for themselves!

Change screams for the simple solution: Do not ask fifty questions, ask *five* essential questions. Then develop a behavioral eagle's eye. I promise you that 90% of the change issues are about ineffective communication or relationship problems. Yes, there are technological mishaps or analytical mistakes, but most of those occur because somebody is failing to communicate, or hoarding information, or is simply misinformed.

Every change warrior knows that simple solutions require sweat. Just like Toto in the Wizard of Oz, you must pull back the curtain of perception (or deception) to show the truth. Suddenly, the change issue is not the floating head with a booming voice and bursts of fire behind it. Instead, it is the small man behind the curtain pulling the levers. Search for the simple, behavioral solution. If you begin to get a sense of what that is in the assessment, it will guide you throughout the rest of the change effort.

CHAPTER VI
Deliver the Teachable Moment

*O*nce an assessment is completed, the change warrior knows that the truth must be delivered to the leader(s) who requested the change. While this sounds easy enough, delivering the truth requires the heart of a lion. Why? Because this is where the fact that "the higher up you go, the less truth you hear" becomes an obstacle to the change warrior delivering the truth. In some situations, you not only have to redefine reality for leaders, you have to reveal that their direct reports may not have been stating the truth all along.

During an initial meeting with a CEO and his second-in-command, I asked them a simple question: "What percentage of your employees do you believe are currently employing the sales behaviors that have been taught over the past year?" The second-in-command, Bob, piped in with total confidence, saying, "My leaders are saying at least 80% of them are using the right behaviors. I think your sales assessment is going to show what an amazing job we're doing right now. I'm excited about it." The CEO seemed to believe Bob, who in turn, totally believed his direct reports from management.

My mind turned into a scale, weighing Bob's words on one scale while balancing his body language on the other. I wondered, *Did he really believe what his direct reports were telling him? Or was he sharing untruths with his CEO to cover his own ass?* I knew they had invested a lot of money in sales training, and since nobody was really out in the field observing anybody, they were all relying on stories told in a bottom-up kind of gossip line.

Remember the game, "Telephone," where you whisper something in somebody's ear and each person passes it along to the next until you go all the way around the room? And by the time the last person delivers the message, it is so far from the original message everybody laughs? Well, imagine this message going all the way around a billion dollar company, while meeting with political pressure along its journey, morphing original messages into company platitudes that sound really good in executive meetings. Those altered messages were what my leaders were basing their perceptions of success on, despite the fact that they had called me in to help raise a stalled sales performance.

"I understand your desire for a positive story out there," I told the CEO and Bob. "You all invested a lot of money in this effort, but I want you to understand that in most situations the application of new behaviors after any training rollout is considerably less than 80%."

Bob looked at me as if I had committed some form of blasphemy. His head cocked slightly to the left, as if he couldn't even take in my comment, then he leaned forward on his elbow and said with a confident smirk, "My leaders don't lie. I believe in them, and you're going to find the truth." He indignantly jabbed the air with his index finger when he said the word *truth.*

Tension filled the room, so I tried to smile in my moment of danger so Bob would know I was on his side. "I have no doubt they believe they are telling the truth," I responded, "but leaders are busy and sometimes don't observe salespeople in action, so they believe the stories they are told." I paused for a moment, then added, "And sometimes those stories are based upon other managers who aren't observing either. But, I'm sure we'll find out the truth, and I appreciate your belief in your leaders."

I felt as if I had just told the Great Wizard of Oz that he was nothing more than Professor Marvel, using smoke and bogus information to make a buck. I didn't mean to do that, because these leaders were honorable ethical men and I hoped their greatest fault was simply believing in those who worked for them. I also knew their deep belief would make my revelations more painful, requiring a pre-meeting cocktail of Tums and caffeine.

Truly, I felt torn; if I found out 80% of the employees were actually doing everything right, then something else was going horribly wrong. If I found out that the usual 15% to 20% were using the sales behaviors properly, I would have to tell the executives that their direct reports were, for some reason, not relaying the truth. I decided that the only thing I could deliver with integrity was the truth — something these two company leaders didn't always hear.

So, I conducted the assessment with no bias on my part; I simply wanted to uncover the truth in order to build an improvement strategy. As a change warrior, you want to conduct assessments so you can work with leaders to determine the specific actions that will make things right. Do not conduct assessments in order to find something wrong. I have always thought that was an important distinction to make.

The company's CEO and sales leader, Bob, asked me to keep them updated on how the interviews were going. Diplomatically, I explained to them why I would rather not do this. Sometimes, information gets back to other leaders and honest answers fall victim to fear of upsetting the CEO. In addition, leaders who cease to hear the truth are partially responsible. Somewhere along the way company leaders let people know — directly or indirectly — they don't want to hear any bad news, so they over praise the good messages and over punish critical messages. In my assessment interviews, I wanted the truth to be as forthcoming as possible. The CEO and the sales leader both had the courage and integrity to agree.

This company was so large the report itself was pretty extensive, even with my streamlined approach. I had conducted hundreds of interviews at all levels and worked with a team to conduct hundreds of observations. After compiling the information, I realized that the truth was closer to what I had anticipated — only 15% to 20% of the employees on the line were actually using the sales behaviors.

Interview responses between levels of leadership within a region were not consistent, which means communication was not good and expectations were not clear. Again, one region had gotten my questions ahead of time and prepared for them. The leaders in that region asked the employees to memorize certain answers to my interview questions, which failed when people forgot their lines while talking to me, and the truth came gushing out.

Leadership's responses were impressive. They said things like, "I think this sales process has made a big difference for my team," or "My team members are disciples of this process, and they are using it every day." However, the observations were not proving those comments to be true. Apparently, sales leaders were finding ways to manipulate sales numbers to ensure that their reports showed sales growth. They had been playing that game for years, and everyone seemed satisfied.

The problem was the company had years of flat earnings, since there was as much going out the back door as coming in the front. The game was over. Now, sales behaviors were their only hope, but they were going the route of insanity by doing the same things they had been doing over the past several years and hoping for a different result. It was time for me to deliver what would be a very tough message.

I had two hours to present what could easily be four hours of information to the CEO and Bob. As presentation time drew near, I walked up to the executive floor, my heart pounding with both anticipation and the effects of two Cokes. A very nice, professional assistant escorted me into the boardroom to wait for the CEO and Bob. The room fit every stereotype of an executive boardroom, including a ridiculously long table and leather chairs that could seat Andre the Giant. A large oil painting of the same gray-haired man who seems to show up in every boardroom hung on the wall. Seated in one of the large leather chairs, I searched for a phone book I could sit on so my chin wouldn't be resting on the table. Before I could locate my booster seat, Bob sauntered in with premature confidence and sat at the head of the table. He looked sideways at me with a knowing smile.

"So," he said, "we have some good results to share?"

I still wondered if he knew the truth and he was hoping I would just succumb to the pressure of presenting to the CEO and give a positive report. I didn't want to get into an in-depth conversation without the CEO, but I did want Bob to have a heads up.

"Well, the news is what it is," I replied. "The good news is that we have a huge opportunity to improve sales results."

Bob fidgeted with his cufflinks. "So, what does that mean?" At that exact moment, the six-foot, four-inch CEO entered the room and sat directly across from me in a chair closest to the two glass doors. We were eye-to-eye with four feet of a walnut table between us.

"Okay, let's get this done," the CEO stated.

Change warriors know there is no time for chitchat with CEOs. So, with those words I began my two-hour reveal. I started by explaining the process so both men understood the importance of why I used interviews and observations. More than 200 retail stores had been involved, and we had completed the process in less than six weeks.

The CEO fidgeted in his chair and looked over the top of his reading glasses at me. "I know how this is done; I don't need to hear about the process. Just give me the results."

In that moment, I realized my well-laid plan of setting up the presentation for greatest impact was over. He wanted to get straight to the data.

"Well, I will tell you that the deduction you all made, based upon leadership reports and conversation, that 80% of the frontline is using the sales skills we trained them on over the past year, is not accurate."

Bob expanded his nervous smile, bouncing his knee up and down under the table until it shook the floor. "So, how far off were we?"

I looked them both in the eye and said, "Based upon in-depth interviews and detailed observations, about 15% of the workforce is actually using the sales behaviors they were taught. The worst percentages came from your middle managers. Some of your managers are using the behaviors less than 10% of the time."

Silence floated down over the conversation. The CEO's face turned red, enraged by the messages his own leaders had given to him. He had grown up with some of these sales managers; they were more than his leaders, they were his friends. He believed in them, and I could see the look of a man betrayed. I wanted to let him know that it was not that the leaders were lying to him; it was that they were not getting out and observing what was really happening. Everybody was giving the story they heard from everybody else. But before I could say any of this, I heard a bang as Bob's knee slammed into the table. I looked at him.

He was leaning toward me with a look that said he wanted to wish me into oblivion. Bob had been the last to promise the CEO great results. I realized from the look on Bob's face that he had truly believed the news from the leaders in the field. His optimism was neither malicious nor conniving, it was simply naive.

I tried to shift the mood by saying, "The good news is, can you imagine the results we can drive if we start to use the behaviors just 30% of the time? We have a huge opportunity for improvement here." Well, my optimism fell totally flat.

I went back to the report, trying to explain what behaviors were missing and the available solutions. Ten minutes into my two-hour presentation, the CEO smacked his hand on the table. "You have ten minutes to finish this report." He had heard enough.

Amazingly, I fit one hour and fifty minutes into ten minutes. I knew the information was the truth they needed to hear to get real change. In fairness to the CEO, he was frustrated but quickly faced the truth. Rather than questioning my findings, he simply accepted them and went into action. Once I finished my final ten minutes, he slammed his report shut, looked at Bob, and said, "We have a lot of work to do." Then, he nodded in my direction and left the room.

I was waiting for the lecture, but Bob, as the second-in-command, was incredibly kind, and commended me for being able to wrap up a two-hour presentation in ten minutes. Bob was anxious to talk to some of the leaders who had promised something they had not delivered. I let him know that many of the leaders thought they had changed their behavior, and believed they had done more than they actually had.

Management was used to living through the newest sales process, while continuing to do things the way they always had and getting by with it. The flat sales results had ended their reign of "this too shall pass." The latest sales initiative had been delivered only through training without a clear plan for putting that training into action. Most of the leaders had implemented behaviors any way they knew how, with very little direction. I commended the sales leaders who had actually gotten some results from their efforts.

While the meeting was tense and the CEO frustrated, that interaction created enough energy to propel the entire sales effort forward. The CEO took personal responsibility for its future success, and every leader was soon given absolute clarity about what success looked like and how it would be measured.

In time, I saw that Bob was a person of integrity who wanted to know the truth and was willing to do what it took to move things forward. We proceeded to build a strong relationship that lasted for more than a decade. We tied the sales effort into every possible initiative to ensure that we were setting up managers and employees for success. Bob and I met almost weekly, and he started calling all of the line leaders weekly to coach them directly. Bob also traveled out to the field, walking into the retail branches of the company to observe what was really going on.

Bob and I worked with the head of communications to ensure that all leadership communication was clear. We also worked with the training director to ensure that communications were partnered with specific behaviors and skills, along with the head of sales to ensure that the behaviors were driving the right results and with the right incentives. Because of these leaders' willingness to work together, we had tremendous success over the next several years.

My relationship with the CEO continued to be occasionally contentious, but always honest. The change eventually became the norm, but it was a painful journey—maybe because this was the rare organization where leaders were both friends and colleagues. What I admired most about the CEO is that he led the change without question, realizing that the results were the results, and something needed to be done.

The moment I had to deliver the unhappy news to the company CEO and the top sales manager was one of my toughest situations because I had leaders who believed they knew the truth. I truly believe that some of the CEO's anger came from the realization that he knew the happy news was not the truth, but he had accepted it in the past in order to avoid facing one more thing that needed to be fixed within his company.

I was also concerned they might have doubted my delivery, dismissing me as a change consultant just trying to drum up work. I left that presentation exhausted, but with the satisfaction that I had delivered a teachable moment that was the necessary truth. During the next several years, the company experienced growth every quarter. That is the potential power of the teachable moment, and a leader who is willing to act on it.

CHANGE LESSON

The Truth

Change warriors know that the real teachable moment must be based upon the truth, otherwise the moment is simply a ruse set up to please the leader. CEOs cannot positively lead their company when decisions are built on the shifting sands of happy messages. While the truth might create initial anger, people seem to know when it is being delivered. The leaders who have been giving the "right" answers even when they are not true are not totally at fault. The CEO had an idea that the behaviors were not really being instituted when more sales were not being made. He knew it did not ring true, but he did not want to have to do anything about it.

Too many consultants and leaders lack the courage to give the tough message. Instead, they offer another vanilla presentation that neither impacts change nor breaks down the status quo — it just keeps the status quo going. A change warrior knows he or she has to state the truth in order to help the company move forward.

CHANGE LESSON

A Case for Action

If an assessment is thorough and accurate, then teachable moments are inevitable. Sometimes, they are extremely positive, and other times, they are uncomfortable. Either type of moment can become a case for action, igniting the change initiative. Even if a leader is reluctant to hear the truth, if he or she is willing to take action then that will make all the difference.

I was fortunate to work with a CEO and a sales leader who took action once I presented the teachable moment. I have had other CEOs tell me, "I don't think your assessment is accurate, and I think we're fine the way we are. We just need a little more training." Any leader who refuses to face the truth will never create tough change in his or her company. Instead, that leader will simply maintain the status quo.

A true change warrior will refuse to stay if a leader resists next-step actions to create necessary change. If a leader is not going to face the truth, then there is no need for a change warrior to stay. Company CEOs and leaders are surrounded with enough yes-people who will go through the motions without any true impact. Change warriors want to make a real difference, not become the court jester for an ego-driven CEO.

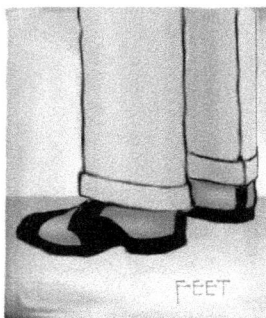

Move the Feet

---

*"It's the most unhappy people
who most fear change."*

Mignon McLaughlin
Journalist and Author

CHAPTER VII

Value Progress Over Popularity

*O*nce a change warrior delivers the teachable moment, there needs to be some preparation for backlash. Up until this point, you were the hired savior who was going to save them from years of neglect. Many CEOs are used to throwing money at problems and only want the report that says, "Your money bought this person who brought this product, which fixed everything." However, as a change warrior, once you deliver the truth to the company leadership, their opinion of you might shift temporarily.

When you are hired to conduct an independent assessment of a company's effectiveness and business behaviors, the CEO and top leaders believe you will make their lives easier, but instead, you might deliver information that creates more work for them. The regional and front-line leaders, who, in the past, counted on the effectiveness of their inspirational stories, might feel exposed when you give your report. If you are doing a courageous job as a change warrior, your observations and interviews will pull back the curtain on their monthly "happy" reports. Depending upon the health of the organization, you will face varying levels of resistance at this point. Those organizations that understand business behaviors and how they impact numbers will be ready to move forward. However, organizations that are used to manipulating numbers without a focus on business behaviors will be especially uncomfortable at this point.

One particular incident following my teachable moment at a company assessment was especially memorable. I had been involved in this company's meetings for about a year as an internal sales consultant. Then they asked me to do an involved assessment of the company's business practices and sales effectiveness. After four months of gathering information through observations and interviews, the retail leader, Stan, called together his twelve top managers to hear my findings and go over a two-hundred-page report I had compiled.

When I entered the executive conference room for the meeting, the familiar faces that usually were smiling and helpful were now glaring at me, looking more like hungry vampires than the congenial bankers with whom I generally interacted. My heart pounded as I gingerly placed my legal pad and pen on the U-shaped conference table that could seat almost sixty people.

I told myself, *Breathe in, breathe out, relax. Surely, I am imagining this intense negative reaction to my recent review of the sales process in this company.* However, everyone at the table knew my final report included a ranking of the regions according to how effectively they were implementing the sales strategy. My ranking of behaviors matched numerical-results ranking precisely and I could not put every regional president in the first place spot. They were aware I had inspected each region closely. In addition, this was the first time this company had really held its leadership team responsible for sales behaviors in addition to sales results.

I reminded myself that I believed in the change process, and I believed the results were fair. Change warriors must deliver unpopular news sometimes, and I was ready for the glares and angry responses. What I wasn't prepared for was the personal rejection that I felt. Other meetings I attended with this group of leaders usually included lots of conversation and laughter, but today there was only the sound of an occasional cough or the clicking keys of a blackberry.

I tried to make eye contact with a few of my closest comrades, but there was no visual reciprocity. They looked down, reviewing their agenda as if it were the latest work of a hot new author. While we all waited for the retail sales leader to arrive, the silent room grew increasingly awkward. I believed this process would turn the sales behaviors around in the company, and soon everybody's results would improve and customers would get better service. So, I ignored the heat slowly filling my face and sat quietly.

Then I heard a chair push back on the Berber carpet, and the unmistakable sound of materials being gathered up from the table. The first of four retail leaders to my right stood slowly and walked behind my chair. She walked past the middle tables to the far left of the U-shape configuration, and then dramatically plopped her materials on that table and sat down.

I tried to smile, but the gesture was not reciprocated, and I wondered when the head of retail would come in and break the hanging cloud of silence. Then I heard it again—squeaky chair wheels on the carpet as yet another retail leader to my right pushed back his chair, picked up his blackberry and notebook, and stood up slowly. He walked across the front of the room to the other side, pulled out a chair next to the last defector, and sat down slowly. His look was a little more apologetic, but was quickly reinforced by a pat on the arm from the woman who had just been seated.

Finally, the retail leader, Stan, entered the room. As he sat down, two more leaders moved to the other side of the room. Now, I sat in a row of twenty chairs all alone. Stan looked at me with some element of surprise, and then began the meeting.

As a change warrior, I was confident with the results of my work. The executive leadership team and I had chosen top performers to go out and observe the retail bank branches, filling out multiple observation sheets for each branch and interviewing every single employee to check for business knowledge and implementation of sales and service behaviors. The observation teams I had formed for this assessment had done an amazing job, and I had spent twelve hours a day for four months compiling the information.

Before Stan could get through Roman numeral one of the agenda, a regional leader asked for permission to make a request. This was a formal move for a pretty informal gathering, so Stan gave him the floor. The message came through loud and clear: "I'd like to suggest that Donna no longer attend our meetings. We don't feel comfortable having her here."

Just when I thought things could not get more uncomfortable in this meeting, they did! Now, I was sitting on one side of the room by myself, being talked about as if I did not exist. Stan looked at the retail leader and then at me with his mouth wide open like a bass out of water. He was as surprised by this turn of events as I was. As Stan tried to figure out what was going on, he calmly asked me, "Donna, could you please leave the room for a moment? Just stand outside, we'll get back to you."

I picked up all of my belongings, feeling a lot like a participant on a reality TV show who has to pack her suitcase before being voted off the show. Standing outside the heavy doors, I heard muffled but raised voices, and I assumed there was a pretty good chance I wasn't going to return. After fifteen agonizing minutes, Stan asked me to return.

"Donna, we have decided that you *do* add value to these meetings, and deserve to be here," Stan said in a friendly voice. "People, Donna just organized the feedback. She's not responsible for the results, you are. You need to give her a break."

I sincerely appreciated the support of the retail leader, and discovered that one or two other leaders had supported me. Quietly, I took my seat, and put on my change warrior armor. I decided to understand the reason for the glares and hold my head high. Change warriors cannot be faint of heart. They have to generate their stand, be sure of their commitment, and then be mentally prepared to take the blows.

Here is what every change warrior must know: To take this kind of pressure you have to have a clear commitment and belief in the stand you have taken. You have to be completely confident in your findings. Here are some points of preparation I made for this particular assessment:

- I immersed myself in the company's sales process, studied it, and determined how it would impact results and service levels. I thought about how customers would benefit from the sales process and how employees would benefit. I believed the company needed to make changes.

- I traveled from region to region to observe each leader and determine who was effective and working hard, and who was sitting in his or her office while self-promoting. I gathered from those visits and interviews that the best leaders also believed that this change was right for the company. Even though they faltered briefly in the controversy, they became the leaders of the future. I believed in them.
- I knew the timing was right for change in this company. Based upon years of being a change warrior, I knew that the leaders had enough pain and commitment to create change. They had been too comfortable for too long. Plus, they now had a new CEO who was willing to do what it took to get results moving in the right direction, especially in a struggling economy. If a shake-up didn't happen, this company was not going to survive. I believed the time was right.

Despite the initial resistance, I ended up developing healthy relationships with these retail leaders. They eventually admitted that the feedback I provided was fair and accurate, and they put their energy into putting their specific sales plans into action. I focused on doing anything that I could to help their teams succeed. This included attending their sales kick-offs, training, and developing any workshops they might need to reinforce their efforts.

Within six month, sales were up 38%, and that was just the beginning of success. The leaders met the change challenge and built a stronger company. They also became better leaders, while I learned the role fear plays in the early stages of change.

Change agents can implement projects and plans, and provide lots of fancy charts and checklists. But to truly change behavior, a change warrior has to realize that he or she is dealing with human beings who bring to every change their own fears, perceptions, and experiences. More importantly, they bring their personal concerns to the table, even if they don't intend to. For instance, maybe the leader who is going to lose his job has been a family friend. Or perhaps the new change is something a leader is sure will push her out of a job she has held since she got out of college.

People react to every change first from the heart. The change warrior must be prepared to handle the pummeling emotional fists of people who are afraid, who feel trapped, and who are scared. Change does not happen because of a perfect plan; change happens because a leader has changed his or her own heart first and is willing to do what it takes to show others *why* the change is right for them.

Remember, emotional pummeling means there is energy. I would rather face a room of furious retail leaders than a room of apathetic ones. Sitting alone on one side of a conference room was not the toughest moment I have faced as a change warrior, but when it happened, I reminded myself of the message I tell leaders who are sponsoring the change: "When employees start to get angry, and resist, and yell at you—celebrate. That means the change is starting to take." The adage "no pain, no gain" is as true for change as anything else. If everyone's happy, nobody's changing!

CHANGE LESSON

Absolute Belief Required

Change warriors must understand that one of the first consequences of change is that you are not going to remain popular—at least for a while. People might love you at first, they might laugh, and jump up and down, and relish in the newfound energy change brings. That is, until change impacts them personally. Once that happens, your popularity will plummet as fast as President Nixon's reputation following the discovery of some tape recordings.

This is why it is so important that you absolutely believe in the change you are bringing to the table. Your belief that this project or process or new leader is the right direction for the company is going to keep you focused when your popularity wanes. If it is more important to be liked than to make sure the company changes, then you are not a change warrior and you need to hand over the reins to someone else. Simply, you can't accept the title "Miss Congeniality" and affect change.

Whenever a change leader basks in the compliments offered during the honeymoon period and believes the hype—he or she is going to fail and it won't be pretty. While people mean well, the compliments you are receiving are either because they think you are going to fix something for them, or they want to hang on to you because you are the popular person. Remember: when your popularity goes, so do they.

CHANGE LESSON

Hang Tough

There are going to be people who attach to you like a barnacle and ride through the change, but that doesn't mean they are supporters. They could be gathering information from you to share with others—and eventually take you down. They could be smiling the biggest but be the most afraid, and subsequently will take every opportunity to make sure your suggested changes don't succeed. Keep in mind that famous saying, "Keep your friends close and your enemies closer." Do not ever assume that those who are smiling and whispering, and closing the door of your office to give you some "inside" information are truly on your side. They might just be your greatest enemies.

Change warriors have to be willing to be unpopular. Why? Because they value progress over popularity. They are willing to sacrifice in the short-term to win for the team, and their lack of popularity will, at some point, turn into tremendous respect from those who were asked to change. As soon as reluctant employees stop their defensive growling and recognize the benefits, they will see you as that tough teacher they hated at first but later respected and appreciated. So hang in there, and surround yourself with a small team that will keep things moving forward while you are taking bullets.

CHAPTER VIII

Find Change Disciples

As a change warrior, you must find those fellow warriors within a company who are willing to take the change journey with you. Being a leader of change does not need to be a lonely job. Once you deliver a teachable moment, it is time to assemble an army of passionate disciples that is ready to implement and reinforce new company behaviors. Finding the right disciples at this point in the journey is absolutely critical. This is a lesson I learned along the way in my own change journey.

I define change disciples as employees who believe in the mission, and who have the skills to carry it out, along with the charisma to help others "catch fire." They also believe enthusiastically that the change mission can be accomplished. These disciples are critical to the success of the change process. Change disciples are the ones who will go out into the field as the company's leaders, reaching places one change warrior working alone simply could not. Often, they have already built trust with people in the company and they can be very effective in promoting the change process. I doubt if there is a change leader in history who accomplished significant change without a group of disciples to make the journey with him or her.

One company I consulted needed a lift in their sales and service results as quickly as possible. I had already conducted an informal assessment, and I had presented the results to the company leadership. My next step was to surround myself with a few change disciples to keep the energy moving forward. I figured I had a few weeks before the enthusiasm would begin to wane.

Toward the end of that honeymoon period, I met with a top leader at the company, Laurel, who believed in the change I proposed and she was willing to do whatever it took to make it happen. Laurel had been with the company for less than a year, so she did not have the emotional albatross of old relationships, or the blinders of being immersed in the situation for too long. Laurel was totally committed to the success of the company.

She was in charge of about forty trainers, and I told her we needed to hand select seven trainers to become our internal sales team. We posted the positions, preparing for the initial onslaught of trainers who wanted out of their current jobs. To avoid attracting those who simply wanted to jump jobs, we made it clear this group of trainers would be the company's version of the reconnaissance Marines. They would be the best of the best, and they would have to be in top emotional condition. We explained that we wanted these special trainers to be the most passionate about sales, and the most willing to be flexible — shifting as needed to serve the mission. Our select group of trainers would serve three key positions:

- Trainers in the classroom;
- Coaches in the field;
- Advisors to leaders in local geographies.

Laurel and I created special questions and scenarios for the interview process in order to gently weed out those who applied for the special trainers' jobs as a means to run away from something rather than move into an exciting, new opportunity. We made it clear to all the applicants that this interview process would be intense, and they needed to be willing to answer some tough questions as well as participate in extemporaneous role plays and lead a sales session in front of an audience.

This was the beginning of boot camp, not because we wanted to make people feel badly about themselves, but because we knew these positions would be demanding. Although this was an exciting opportunity, we warned applicants it could be lonely at times. As change leaders, these special trainers would experience times of unpopularity with employees and leaders.

From past experience, I had learned to be wary of change disciples who ultimately only had their own best interests at heart, not the company's. Only once did I end up with a disciple who was more concerned about his own success than that of the change initiative. He ended up being an incredible stumbling block, looking only for opportunities of self-promotion and turning on the change initiative when one powerful leader enticed him with promises of a leadership position. Disciples have to be more focused on others than on themselves, so Laurel and I were highly attuned to any applicants who simply wanted the job.

The presentation of the position ultimately provided us with the change warrior apprentices—the disciples—we needed. Laurel and I found our magnificent seven who were about to accelerate the whole process faster than even I had imagined.

As a change warrior, I knew that in order to move forward, we would have to remove the excuses that were blocking the company's path to success. I told the new sales trainers that we wanted to eliminate the excuses provided by leaders who hoped to prove that the new sales process would not work. I had been in the field as a salesperson, so I knew that many of management's reasons for low sales results were legitimate. However, the problem was not with those on the frontline interacting with customers every single day. Often, the problem was the leaders who were not providing coaching and leadership. Leaders were sitting in offices running numbers while their service and sales people were doing what was asked of them, and doing it pretty darn well considering the fact that they were not told how to get better results.

Laurel and I decided to pick a few key leaders we knew who would put all of their energy into the change efforts, and have the new sales trainers coach them. We needed one change leader in every type of market so we could say, "Regardless of market type, this process works."

The company's current sales results were not going to sustain this company for much longer, and my job was to do what it took to get movement in the right direction. Our first job with the special trainers' team was to educate them on what needed to happen to make the needed changes needed. We assigned each of them to a local bank branch and for a week, they observed every job at the bank and only asked questions if it helped them understand the job more completely. Similar to current TV reality shows where the boss goes "undercover," our sales trainers did the same. Just like the CEOs on reality shows who are transformed by what they observe, our warriors were amazed by what they found.

The seven special trainers soon found out that things were not as predictable in the field as their earlier role-plays in the classroom depicted. They started to see the challenges of employees facing unhappy customers, or trying to find answers to confusing problems, and leaders who were not present to guide their employees. The trainers also met people who were working incredibly hard and needed their assistance. The trainers started to feel a true sense of purpose in their roles as a coach and guide. Now, they knew there were employees they were going to help succeed. During that week of observation, all seven special trainers became "heart engaged."

After their week in the field, Laurel and I gave them extensive training on how to coach employees and leaders. Each trainer had a clear, simple plan they would build around a couple of key business behaviors. They would coach the employees and leaders on effectively using these behaviors until the sales numbers started to lift. Simultaneously, we took them through "train-the-trainer sessions," to make sure each trainer delivered the same experience. We also brainstormed the most common objections employees and leaders would offer, and practiced our responses so everyone was delivering the same message.

The most amazing benefit was the ability to bring real-life examples of coaching successes and failures into the classroom. The trainers learned how to use their real-life experiences to deal with participants who balked at learning a new skill, explaining, "That sounds great in here, but it will never work in the real world." Because of the trainer's actual coaching experience, they could respond to the resistance, saying, "Well, actually it did work in the real world with a branch I entered last month. They've had 30% growth because of this behavior." Believe me, those moments are every change warrior's dream.

Carefully preparing change disciples has the added advantage of knowledgeable trainers working in the branches. Many employees had not been through the training, or had managers who were failing to coach. Our trainers entered the work environments with the best knowledge of the company's sales process and they applied that knowledge by preparing plans with simple actions.

I spoke to the trainers almost every single day, and each week Laurel and I met by phone with the seven trainers for a team meeting. They were our change disciples — spreading their knowledge throughout the company, conquering with competence, and guiding with wisdom. Management learned to value these special trainers and often requested that one or two come back to their region. The training director, Laurel, actually started being invited to line leader meetings because management realized the value of correctly implemented training.

As a result of our efforts to cultivate change disciples at this particular company, some branches saw a 100% lift in sales within a six-to-twelve-week period. The trainers hit some rough patches, for sure. For example, some trainers would walk into a branch and the manager would arrange to be gone for the week they were there. Or, they had leaders who wanted to pin their poor leadership on our trainers. The change disciples did experience the loneliness of consultants with lots of days on the road and a new group of employees to help or to teach every week. However, the change disciples made it work because they believed in the process; they believed in the leaders; and they knew they were making a difference.

Every change job I have ever worked on, I look early for my change disciples. I know they will be an extension of my change initiative, reaching out to provide the skills and information employees need to help the organization succeed. I have used this approach with product overhauls, communication efforts, service quality efforts, and sales process initiatives. The type of project does not matter. It is about reaching out to human beings and improving their lives by sharing simple skills and coaching them along the way. Guaranteed: If you improve the lives of your employees, they will improve your organization.

CHANGE LESSON

Change Disciples Are Essential

Change disciples are the experts through whom you will funnel the change effort. A change warrior needs change disciples for three key reasons:

- They know the company from the inside out and they have built trust through relationships.
- They can disperse the change faster by becoming conduit-like tentacles for the change effort.
- They become a strong support system for a change warrior. They link arms and make the journey less lonely and a lot more exciting.

When you select change disciples, do so carefully and with a lot of thought. Do not be fooled by those who have a greater passion for climbing the company ladder than committing to company change. Self-promoters will only be looking out for their own best interests and will likely turn on you just as your mission is gaining momentum.

Choose those who are willing to work hard for the change process and who care more for the people they are helping than the platform that it might provide them. Change disciples will gain acknowledgment and praise if they do their job well, but their delight should always be in the success of others.

CHANGE LESSON

Disciples Bridge the Gap

Change warriors must choose change disciples within the company who know the heart of the work environment. This is critical, especially for an external change warrior. The disciples' ability to keep their finger on the pulse of people's concerns and successes will be invaluable to you as a change warrior.

Once change disciples have learned about the specific challenges of the work environment, make sure they know the skills required for changed behavior better than anyone. The adage, "If you ever want to really understand a subject—teach it," holds true for change disciples. They teach the skills and then help others apply them in the real world. Then, they stay with the teams until change begins to happen, and ultimately stick.

Change disciples are the bridge between knowing and doing, the bridge between what must be done and what is really being done. They take away the "noes," and they provide the wins needed to take the wind out of the sails of naysayers. As all great leaders have discovered, the right disciples are priceless.

CHAPTER IX

Provide Quick and Simple Wins

*T*horeau said it best in *Walden* when he wrote, "Simplify, simplify." In business, we somehow make such detail-laden plans they are almost impossible to put into action. Rather than pulling together a simple plan for the entire company, management tends to separate into markets and regions. Then the powers that be develop a type of corporate rugby game with everybody in a giant scrum, pushing against one another and hoping they get a chance to get the ball at some point. The business world's ability to take a spark of an idea and turn it into a destructive, flaming blaze is amazing.

As a change warrior, I have found that most corporate initiatives begin with the right intent and initially involve the right people. What happens after that reminds me of the sixth grade when I went to recess. There were six, foursquare stations, and only four really good balls available on the ball cart. The best one was a yellowed volleyball that was always firm and allowed great corner shots. About twenty kids were determined to get those four balls since the person who got a ball became a foursquare captain. You can imagine twenty sweaty kids charging across the playground, trying to get to that ball cart first. Once there, a mass of hands and arms would get entangled, body slams ensued, and someone ended up crying. Whoever emerged from the scrum with the yellow volleyball was not the hero, but now the most hated person on the playground. That person ended up with a target on his or her back.

Similarly, that is often the problem I see with corporate initiatives. Rather than an integrated offense where a few leaders are clearly selected, we allow people to charge the ball cart, all grabbing for the same initiative. Once every department in the company has a piece of the initiative, the strategy becomes this incongruous ball of ideas, rolling down a precipitous hill, gaining speed and size, and ultimately, running over employees rather than giving them direction. What should have been a simple directive is now a tangled coalition of plans that is so confusing it is not implementable.

A change warrior knows that once an assessment has been delivered, and change disciples identified, it is critical to deliver the change initiative in terms of simple actions to ensure that everyone knows exactly what to do next.

One of my clients had bought into a very expensive service quality program, but was seeing absolutely no change in customer survey scores. She was terrified that the millions of dollars she had put into the initiative would eventually cost her more than money. At that point, she contacted me. Immediately, I went into the field to talk to leaders, trying to determine what was working and where the obstacles might be.

I gathered enough information to make an assessment on the strengths of the field, along with ideas on how to build on those strengths. I strongly believe that identifying a company's existing strengths excites the leaders to move forward with change. It is easier to get more energy from something already in motion than try to beat on a stationary behavior and push it forward. But it is also critical to recognize if there are any stumbling blocks that need to be removed. Unfortunately, many stumbling blocks are incorrectly identified, and a lot of effort goes into fixing the wrong things.

After a series of interviews and visits, I determined there were two key issues that had become major stumbling blocks. First, the initial training had offered enough actions to last several years, which basically overwhelmed employees as to what to do next. Second, since the employees were overwhelmed, each region had decided to create its own version of the actions, adding even more details to the process.

I spent years as a corporate trainer, so I am not attacking the way the previous training was handled. Believe me, I have been the trainer in front of the room trying to get a company's employees through five months' worth of information in one day. Training directors know that the time allowed in front of a large audience is limited; company leaders tend to complain about their employees being out of the office for a lot of training time, especially when they are understaffed. Therefore, instead of doing incremental training on certain actions, they try to cram a year's worth of actions into a one-and-a-half day session.

Once trainers complete a training session, employees leave overwhelmed with a glazed look and a sudden inability to remember anything. In the meantime, the training department reports their "good news" to leadership, stating that everyone had been trained and the employees were ready to implement the new actions. Then leadership says, "Thank God that's over," and marks it off their "make corporate happy" checklist.

Here is the problem with this approach — if a hundred possible actions have been introduced, which ones should be used first?

Each separate regional leader faces this question by adding more confusion to the already enigmatic situation. In fairness, they are concerned about the employees' glazed looks after a training session. Often, when a manager asks an employee how the training day went, he or she might only remember lunch, or how the eraser board markers smelled like different fruit, or maybe winning a free candy bar. Basically, they don't remember much of the training, so leaders try to make some sense of it all by pulling together their own team to try and tackle a rollout that is specific to their region.

With this particular company, I found that leaders had taken the overwhelming list of behaviors introduced in training and created an even longer list by adding their own. Suddenly, five actions had become twenty-five actions. Once I added up all of the different strategic plans at this company, I found hundreds of actions taking place in a variety of regions, many of which were completely different. Not only were the actions varied, but also at some point, each region needed technology support, human resources support, and training support. The staff teams had to assign people to support diversified approaches that were meant to support the same initiative. Everybody had piled on, and a large part of my job as a change warrior was to untangle and simplify the initiative.

For some reason, company leaders often resist simplification. I am not sure if they think a simple strategy won't work, or if they have been brainwashed after years of complex projects to believe complex is better. Perhaps management worries that a super-simple strategy can be more easily tracked than a complex one. There are always a few leaders who know how to bury themselves in complexity so nobody can uncover the ruse.

Whatever the reason for the complexity in this situation, I knew I had to talk with the leaders. So, I went out into the field to determine how we could all come together under one banner. In my first regional meeting, I was thrown a curve ball I had not expected—this group told me they did not see the real advantage in coming together under the corporate umbrella. Subsequently, I found this to be true with almost every regional leader within the company. I realized the big corporate world of mergers and acquisitions had cost employees something really important—their sense of individuality. Each of these regions desperately wanted to contribute their *own* ideas and spin on the service quality actions. They did not want to blend in under the corporate umbrella. They wanted to stand out.

In the past, many in regional management had a negative experience with corporate headquarters. Usually, somebody in a staff position "picked their brain" for ideas then took what he or she gathered and presented it as his or her own ideas. This is a common occurrence, so I understand why some regional employees and leaders see the corporate umbrella as something to avoid. Once it became apparent what was going on with this company, I knew I had to help each region put its individual fingerprint on the strategic plan or the regions would never move forward.

The biggest issue within each region was a lack of focus around which specific actions could be built. Actions without a destination turn into endless meetings going nowhere and creating futile plans. A destination without actions becomes a beautiful palace with no visitors.

I brought the regional leaders together for a group meeting. I asked them to answer two questions:

1) If we only implemented three behaviors, which three would have the greatest impact?
2) Are we willing to say that we will do these three things better than any of our competitors?

Once we had alignment around the three behaviors, I told the leaders we would offer one simple communication tool that would provide tips, successes, and product information — everything the field would need to drive these three behaviors. The company newsletter would help reinforce a new, company-wide language that would provide verbal efficiency. There would be a series of service quality terms that would mean the same thing in every single region. In addition, the newsletter would ensure that information would support the three behaviors and keep people from straying to another behavior. We also decided to print success stories in the newsletter from every region if they could be substantiated by results.

Next, each of the regional leaders had two weeks to deliver a simplified plan to support the training and coaching of each of the skills. Many in the company's corporate headquarters had assumed the regional leaders would fight the established behaviors and want to add some of their own. Oddly, the exact opposite happened. The regional leaders seemed relieved to have a simpler point of focus so they could begin to give better guidance to their employees and track the results.

Two weeks later, each regional leader delivered his or her plan in a single group meeting. We determined which actions reinforced each other, deleted any that would require different technology or training, and shared best practices. We all left that meeting with a two-page strategic plan that drove our three behaviors, which we described in company language that everyone understood and agreed to. Now, we could build technology that supported just a few specific behaviors, educate staff groups so they could support the behaviors, and ensure that goals and incentives reinforced the right behaviors.

The regional leaders' commitment to one another was to stick with these strategic plans until they saw significant lift in results. Once they mastered the three behaviors and became the best in the industry, then they would raise the ante with additional company behavior changes.

I worked with the regional leaders around their commitment to focus on three specific behaviors, and then we set up some ways to celebrate quick victories. This was essential because it would give everybody a winning feeling, which in turn, provided energy to sustain their focus and commitment when they hit plateaus and change became less exciting. Think about people on a weight-loss program, their biggest weight loss is usually in the first couple of weeks. What if they started their diet and only lost one pound in two weeks? Most would quit. But when they see a five, ten, or twelve-pound loss in the first couple of weeks, suddenly, they have a stronger commitment to reach the goal. Quick victories are critical.

Here are a few things we did to jump-start our new strategies:

- I partnered with the two most committed, talented regional leaders and sent training coaches to their branches to help create quick lift. The coaches helped the managers develop a simple action plan for behavior change that improved customer service behaviors. They spent six weeks observing employees and helping the managers ensure the behaviors were implemented. They made note of obstacles to improvement as well as the best, most effective practices. We shared and followed those obstacles and successes in our weekly newsletter and in leadership meetings.

- We made sure that every manager within the company knew what we were doing. We offered a two-to-three-hour class for any corporate leader who was interested that explained our focus and strategies. Many regional leaders offered their support and developed similar plans, creating energy throughout the organization.

- We built a marketing campaign around greeting customers and asking questions to ensure their needs were met during a visit to the bank. We provided scripts for the employees to use when assisting customers, including how to respond to any possible objections they might face. Training included practice sessions to build confidence, and even the employees' smallest successes were recognized and celebrated.

- We developed a day at the end of the change campaign when corporate management observed every branch and measured the service skills and the customer satisfaction. Management also looked at the sales results as a gauge for the campaign's success. The two are always directly related, and when this proved to be true, branch leaders handed out employee awards and reported employee successes to the CEO.

During this jump-start period, I worked with top management to develop a strategy for company leaders to visit branches, offer encouragement, and coach their managers who reported directly to them. In fact, the CEO began holding a weekly service-quality conversation with leaders who reported directly to him. The results of these weekly meetings cascaded throughout leadership. I remember telling one leader, "Within four months, everybody in this company will be talking about service quality and sales results. I promise."

I loved the day he said to me, "You are true to your word. The energy around this initiative is amazing." Those are the moments that sustain change warriors.

CHANGE LESSON

Simplify, Simplify

Sometimes the complexity organizational leaders bring to change initiatives reflects frantic movement rather than a purposeful direction. In addition, we are all so busy making sure we have put our "stamp" on an initiative that we end up confusing the employees who actually have to put one foot in front of the other, usually in front of a customer. Change warriors need to help management fall out of love with complex project plans that look impressive in meetings. Instead, change warriors can help clients fall in love with simple, two-page plans that drive actual results.

At the same time, change warriors must acknowledge that the people of each region are proud of their ideas, and want to know that they have, in some way, impacted the project. This is not because people need attention; it is because they want to contribute to those around them. A change warrior knows how to go out into the field and see what regional branches are doing first, then bring them together to determine how the many plans can become the few successful ones. This way, each region is represented, and all are engaged in the effort.

CHANGE LESSON

Successful Quick Hits

A change warrior's greatest challenge will be harnessing people's energy to move forward and sustain it throughout the change process. As a change warrior, your first actions and points of victory must be celebrated in an exaggerated fashion, since you will need the adrenaline when things are not quite as easy in the future. At some point, those positive experiences will sustain employees' enthusiasm when change doesn't go so well. A change warrior will remember the wins, keep a file of why they worked, and surround him or herself with the company leaders who still believe in the change process.

More importantly, quick wins make true believers out of those who are asked to change. Most people want proof that something works before they are willing to jump on board. Some have been burned in the past by jumping on an initiative that went out the door with a leader who left the company. Others have put enormous time into a change project that just inexplicably disappeared. You have to make people believe you know what you are talking about. A change warrior's dramatic effect is wrapped up in the quick hits that declare this is not just another bogus initiative that gets no results and only takes time. This works.

Light a Fire

"Loyalty to petrified opinions never yet broke a chain or freed a human soul."

Mark Twain

American Author and Humorist

CHAPTER X

The Courage to Change

*O*nce upon a time there was a corporate change warrior who conducted an informal assessment, revealed the truth, gathered disciples, got things moving, and they all lived happily ever after.

Yes, that would have to begin with "once upon a time" because it would definitely be a fairly tale. A company leader might hope that once a change warrior has done all of the above that the hard part is over, but it is not. Those initial quick wins are just that — they are quick, and they are usually minor in the bigger picture of change, yet they are majorly celebrated.

So, while most people in the organization are celebrating the quick win, the change warrior understands this is only the starting point. Now, the change warrior must use the energy created by the quick win as fuel for the real journey.

When the change initiative has some momentum, it is time to declare an acceleration in change. This helps prepare employees for more hard work in order to reach the company's goals for change. While the honeymoon period fades quite quickly once a change warrior delivers the news about hard work, it definitely disappears when real change starts impacting a larger number of people.

As a preacher's kid, I learned how to lead change by observing my parents in their roles as spiritual change makers. In fact, my father, who was a minister, usually accepted the call of churches that were struggling. He rebuilt them, and within two to three years our family would move on. I was always amazed by my parents' incredible willingness to lead change, since rarely did they come out the other side without battle scars.

During the honeymoon phase at a new church, my parents familiarized themselves with the congregants, determined the change disciples, and created positive movement. Then, they gathered their energy because they knew it was time to buckle up for the bumpy ride of what they called "Phase Two." As the minister, my father prepared intensely for this second phase because he knew people tended to run amuck if not given clear direction.

To eliminate surprises while announcing the need for courage and energy, my father would deliver what we would affectionately call "that sermon." This would be the sermon that would boldly announce the church's new mission, while touching on a core change issue. This would be the sermon that would cause a sea of smiling faces in the congregation to suddenly turn to fear or disapproval.

My dad would develop "that sermon" to fit the need of the current congregation, honing his sermon to an actionable mission statement. His delivery directly addressed the particular issue that stood in the way of the church's forward movement as a spiritual community. In addition, his sermon would hit the heart of an uncomfortable truth, and do it in a way that would not cause a mass exodus.

Usually, the night before my dad would deliver "that sermon" to a congregation at Sunday services, our family would have an extra long prayer at dinner, and then spend the evening laughing as much as possible. We thought of it as the comedy before the storm. Generally, we would watch Mary Tyler Moore, Bob Newhart and Carol Burnett (stars of the staple comedy shows of 1970s Saturday night television) and laugh nonstop because we knew we were going to be sitting in hot water the next day.

The morning of "that sermon" included lots of gallows humor in my family. We would debate if we should all dress in black and carry sickles, or simply provide the congregation with eggs and let them have at us during the altar call. When my dad would give the tough sermon about change, the congregants would usually be quite unhappy with my family. Most Sundays, my family members would divide up and each of us would sit with friends, but on this day our family stayed a unit, marching into church with smiling faces and the psychological weapon of optimism.

I remember one church in particular that struggled with reaching out to the financially poor. The congregants were willing to feed and clothe the needy from a distance, but they didn't want them to actually show up in their beautiful sanctuary and depress them on Sunday morning. At the time, my father was working on an advanced seminary degree, and his final assignment for his program created the perfect sermon and teachable moment for this congregation's difficulties with reaching out to the poor.

My father's seminary class had been discussing mission work, so the seminary professor brilliantly decided to help the ministers apply their knowledge. He told the ministers he would give each of them one quarter—25 cents—and they had to live on the streets of San Francisco for three days as a homeless person. In addition, the professor instructed each minister not to bathe or shave for a week prior to living on the street as a homeless person. My dad was really nervous about the potential dangers of this assignment, but anxious to understand what being homeless might feel like.

As it turned out, my father was a terrible beggar. After two days, he had bought one cup of coffee with his quarter and received less than a dollar from begging. He was now both homeless and starving. Later, he would describe how uncomfortable he felt approaching people, and how shocked he was because so many people refused to even look at him. He said a smile would have encouraged him, but the diverted eyes made him feel invisible.

On his last morning as a homeless man, my father stood hungry and exhausted outside of a Christian church, certain he had finally found a place where someone would offer to help him. On that Sunday morning, he watched every single church member walk past him, but not one person made eye contact or offered to help the unshaven, hungry man standing in front of them.

Later that day, my father went to a soup kitchen and met other homeless people. He found them to be nothing like the stereotype of the lazy person who refuses to work for a living. One man had been a college professor when his wife and daughter were killed in a fire. He had simply lost the will to do anything. A woman who worked at the soup kitchen was bipolar and did not have access to the medical help she needed. He met teenagers who had run away from abusive homes and single mothers who were working three jobs, but couldn't afford daycare and were afraid of losing their children to social services. They were all decent human beings who had fallen on hard times.

On his last night on the streets, my father sat against a wall, feeling defeated. Then he heard the voice of a Good Samaritan: "Sir, would you like to join me for dinner?" A sailor, recently disembarked from his ship, held a hand out to help my father get up off the ground. Respectfully, he introduced himself to the homeless man as if they were business colleagues. The sailor did not take him to the local fast food venue for something to go, but instead, took him out for a steak dinner at a nice restaurant. A lot of people stared as they walked through the restaurant, my father smelling like someone who hadn't bathed in ten days and looking just as unappetizing. The sailor acted as if they were best friends and they spent hours in conversation. The sailor told my father he didn't believe in God, but my dad later told his seminary colleagues the young sailor provided the most memorable experience in his three days of homelessness.

After completing his mission, my father maintained his homeless look for another seven days, much to my family's olfactory disgust. We made him stand in the garage and/or backyard a lot that week. I think my father used that alone time to prepare a sermon that would put the angst in the church's change initiative.

Sunday morning finally arrived, and the sanctuary was filled with members anxious to see their minister in the pulpit again. There was a buzz of energy and anticipation.

What the congregants didn't realize was that their minister was already in their presence. He had quietly entered the sanctuary about five minutes earlier, wearing dirty clothes, sporting a beard, greasy hair, a baseball cap, sunglasses—and a lot of body odor. He had plopped down beside a nicely coiffed woman in her fifties who promptly stood up and moved.

Then, my father stood up and moved up the aisle a few more pews. Those who noticed "the homeless man" immediately began to whisper as he passed by them. Who was this person? Was he going to be allowed to ruin the minister's first Sunday back? He proceeded to sit down by a church family who had hosted our family for dinner several times. Their five-year-old son seemed unphased when the homeless man sat near him; the boy looked up, smiled, and kept coloring his picture on the back of the church bulletin. The parents, however, quickly scooted down the pew to the other end, putting lots of space between their son and the homeless man.

I watched in amazement as my father smiled, and moved one more time. As he moved down the aisle, those who noticed him turned their heads and broke eye contact, lest he come their way. The congregation had joined ranks, and my father as a homeless man was having no luck breaking the frightened grip they had formed. His final destination was the front pew, where he plopped down beside the two deacons. At the same time, the music director walked into the church with the choir and the whispers faded into silence.

As the minister of music took his assigned spot to the right of the pulpit, everyone got quiet, as if a jury had just entered the courtroom with a verdict. The minister of music was the only one (besides us) who knew what was going on.

He sat in silence, smiling at the congregation, while people started looking around, laughing nervously, waiting for their minister to pop out of the pulpit like a jack-in-the-box. Then the homeless man in the front pew slowly stood and walked up the steps to the pulpit. The congregants' anticipatory smiles melted into disapproving frowns. The deacons started to stand as if they had considered tackling him before he made it to the top step. Luckily, my dad outpaced them. He faced the choir briefly, and then turned to face the congregation.

Even as his child, I doubted that it was my father in front of that church. He stood at the pulpit, owning the space, pausing for several seconds so everyone could feel the discomfort. Then, he smoothly removed his sunglasses, placed his hands on either side of the pulpit with authority, and leaned into the microphone. He uttered one simple word, "Hello."

The congregation let out a collective gasp. The silence felt so potentially explosive no one even dared to cough. "Hello." That one word was the emotional tripwire, and it could have been his entire sermon.

My father knew this church struggled with those who wanted it to be a mission church and those who wanted it to be a country club, so he told his story with no judgment. He did not preach a sermon, but simply told his story. This approach allowed the congregation to deduce the message each of them needed to hear without finger pointing or blame.

So, "that sermon" announced a ratcheting up of mission work for this particular church in a way that touched the congregants' hearts and souls. Instead of feeling threatened, the church members all became engrossed with their minister's sermon, which was actually a story telling session. My father also provided a map for putting this church's mission into action. Because he first touched their hearts and souls, his congregation was more open to hearing about the significant changes.

I was a teenager at the time and made numerous mental notes on the effectiveness of my dad's honest storytelling, and his ability to move beyond people's defenses and rigid positions on issues. Those lessons have served me well in my own work as a change warrior. I understand how stories allow people to get out of their heads and into their hearts and their imaginations. Perhaps this is why I love telling stories when I have to give "that sermon" to company employees facing change. My "congregants" are the employees in a company who desperately need to make changes in order to thrive.

In business, too often leaders miss opportunities to share powerful stories on a heart and soul level that illustrate essential points for change. Sharing a story reveals something about the speaker, and most leaders don't like that vulnerability. Instead, leaders end up with boring kick-offs coupled with boring speeches that explain what the change is about, but fail to motivate the employees. Change warriors know that change escalation must be announced in a way that evokes passion, and clearly communicates that the status quo at the company is gone. Storytelling can soften "that sermon" and inspire employees to take the next hard steps for change.

As a change warrior, you have the tough job of helping a company's leaders and employees understand that the change plan is going to get more challenging. You also have to offer them a clear roadmap. Many employees resist change because the leaders fail to announce the intensified workload, and when it happens, employees are surprised. As Darryl R. Connor, author of *Managing at the Speed of Change*, observes: "It's not the surprises in life that are so debilitating. The truly crushing force is being surprised that you are surprised."

When you have to give "that sermon," watch for physical reactions in the room, such as people leaning forward, or folding their arms across their chests. Pay attention to raised eyebrows, smiles, or frowns. If you see an audience response, you know people are getting the message. Being able to announce change with stories and passion ensures it is not only heard, but also emotionally digested.

CHANGE LESSON

Announce a Shift in Intensity

Do not make the mistake of assuming that a few quick wins means the hard part is done. Change warriors know this honeymoon period begins with a few optimistic steps and successes inspired by quick wins. During the honeymoon, you create enough energy for employees so they can accept the announcement of the longer lasting, more challenging change effort.

Based upon what you have learned in your initial assessment, determine what the core change issue will be for the company. Then begin to chip away at it with a strong initial message upon which you will build other messages. If there is one thing people resist more than change itself, it is any change that surprises them. Therefore, every leader must announce the company's shift in intensity, and clearly acknowledge this change will require more diligence in order to bring results. Employees also deserve to know that discomfort is a part of the deal.

Announcing a shift in intensity shows the commitment of leadership, because it says, "We're willing to be uncomfortable for a while to achieve this particular goal."

CHANGE LESSON

Touch the Heart

A message that announces a shift in intensity is going to have to engage listeners who might be fearful or just plain resistant. Nothing is more comforting to our frantic psyches than a story. When we hear, "Let me tell you a story," we usually breathe a sigh of relief, relax, and listen attentively. From the time we were small children, we have understood the value of a good story and intuitively have understood it is communication that comes from the heart. Therefore, any change warrior getting ready to share a difficult message needs to include a story that touches the listeners' hearts.

If you only offer rational reasons for accelerating change, you will be met with well-meaning nods of agreement from people who emotionally are still hostage to the old, familiar ways of doing business. The heart has to be okay with the change that is about to happen. Otherwise, people will not have enough energy to implement the changes and stick with them.

Stories allow audiences to derive the message needed without lectures that create defensiveness. In addition, stories touch a certain truth in people's hearts that reminds them of what is important.

CHAPTER XI

People Still Follow the Leader

"We should lead these training sessions." The comment sounded innocent enough, except that it came from the CEO of a top bank. I had been working as an external consultant with this bank's management for almost a year on a variety of projects, and we were getting ready to roll out a new sales initiative. I had developed a training program based on the bank's key measurements for the year and essential critical behaviors some leaders agreed on. We also had a strong training director supporting the initiative, along with several trainers we hand-selected, who had the knowledge and energy to kick this initiative off with a bang.

Thrilled by the clear sign of leadership support, I needed to verify who might be leading these training sessions. When the CEO had commented, "We should lead these training sessions," I was confused.

"Well, who are you referencing when you say 'we'?" I asked the CEO tentatively.

He replied, "I mean, the top leaders in this company, including me, along with the Head of Retail, and our regional leaders. If they're going to say they support this initiative, then they should teach it."

That moment was probably one of my lowest as a change warrior. Instead of jumping onboard, thrilled with the CEO's willingness to really lead, I hesitated. All I could imagine was a roomful of people watching these silver-haired gentlemen read from a scripted leader's guide. I knew that several of the CEO's leaders were not enthused with the proposed changes even though they had aligned themselves with the change plan. My concerns ranged from the company leaders' presentation skills to malicious compliance, where their body language would let the audience know the presenter was ambivalent about the entire change process.

I left the meeting and went to lunch with the Director of Training, Mike. We looked like we had won the lottery but had no idea what to do with so much money. The CEO was handing us an incredible gift of sponsorship, but it could be a gift that might ruin the entire kickoff. Our reaction was an absolute testament to the theory that sometimes change warriors resist change—even when it is positive! Over lunch we brainstormed, thinking about how we could make this work, and how we could help the CEO break the news to his regional directors that they would be leading training sessions.

Finally, Mike and I decided to suggest to the CEO that each regional bank leader be paired with one of our hand-selected trainers to lead one session. That would allow the leaders to show their sponsorship of the change initiative while having help during the session. Many people think training is something anybody can do well, which is not true. The best trainers know how to influence, generate energy, ensure specific actions, and create absolute clarity—all at the same time. We knew the bank's regional leaders would be short on these skills.

When Mike and I met with the CEO and delivered our brilliant solution to have a leader/trainer team teach one session, the CEO responded, "No, that's not enough."

Our hearts dropped. Then I asked, "How might you change the plan?"

"Well, we either do this right or we don't," he responded. "Each leader teaches as many sessions as it takes to get through their entire region. They need to have their face in front of their people because people will follow them." Then he emphasized, "Every person in their region needs to know they cared enough to come to them. I'm okay with pairing them up with a trainer, but I want them to train every session."

In that moment, my respect for the CEO grew considerably as I realized his entire motivation was to show employees in the field that their leaders cared enough to show up. This CEO also knew that nothing would ensure success faster than the regional leaders telling their employees they believed in the process.

The training director and I had stressed the importance of sponsorship, and the CEO was ready to take the first step in supporting our plan for change. We decided to visit all five regions in one day, so the day was jam-packed with with highly energetic, quick meetings. This was my first flight on a corporate jet, and I learned an important CEO lesson immediately. When I sat down across from the tall CEO whose knees were up under his chin, I shook his hand and commented, "Sorry if I seem nervous, I'm a little claustrophobic in small spaces." The CEO quickly defended his jet, and then looked out the window, avoiding further eye contact. I learned to never comment on the size of a man's corporate jet!

Everyone knew the schedule, so things were exciting in a hurried way. Each region had sent a driver to meet us on the airport tarmac, and drive us to that regional headquarters. Each regional leader greeted us politely, shook hands, and offered us seats in the leather chairs across from his massive desk. Immediately, the CEO looked in the eye of each regional leader and said, "You know what this is about. We're getting ready to undertake a significant change with this sales process. Are you on board with it? Are you ready to lead it?"

Each one said, "Yes," without hesitation. Then we quickly left and headed back to the jet for the next stop. We visited five states in one day. I was impressed with the CEO when he took the time in the car to talk with every driver, finding out about each one's life and what he or she did for the company. He listened intently to every response, and continued the conversation until we arrived at our destination. His personable style made the drivers feel both appreciated and respected.

Once we had met with all the regional leaders, we boarded the plane for the trip home. The CEO had warmed up after the size debacle, and he offered me a boxed lunch that contained a sandwich, potato salad, and a brownie. We were sitting across from each other, eating on a small swing out tabletop. We both stared at our potato salad realizing there were no eating utensils in the box lunches. "Well," the CEO said with a smile, "I guess we have to eat this potato salad without a fork."

I was up for the challenge, so I removed the top of the plastic container and dug in with my fingers, laughing softly because I was going to watch a CEO eat with his fingers, too. Well, I thought that was the case. I looked up briefly, potato salad all over my fingers, to see he had fashioned a spoon from the plastic top and was scooping it out gently. Since there was no salvaging this situation, I simply said, "You did that on purpose." He burst out laughing, and I knew this was revenge for my small plane comment at the beginning of the day.

Once we had received verbal commitments from every regional leader, we arranged a "train-the-trainer" session, which they were all required to attend. We selected fifteen leaders to teach the session. In addition to the regional leaders, we also trained the CEO, the Director of Retail, the Head of Marketing, the Director of Sales, and the Director of Training. All the trained leaders partnered with our sales trainers to lead the coaching sessions.

There was one small glitch, however. Although we had notified the leaders that they were to attend the coaching class, they had not yet been informed that they were actually going to *teach* the classes to their employees. As leaders entered the room that morning, one-by-one, I knew from their body language that most were already frustrated they had to attend the training session at all. I knew their reluctance would escalate when the CEO made the big announcement that they would also be teaching.

The Director of Training, Mike, kicked off the session by thanking everyone for being there, and commended each leader for being willing to attend the very session his employees would be attending. Then Mike passed the baton to the CEO, who stood to deliver the news that would delight a few and confound the majority.

"Gentlemen," he began, "thank you for coming to this session. While each of you will be attending this session as a participant, I want you to know that as the key leaders of this company, I'm going to expect you to play a much bigger role in this initiative."

Since many of them were not crazy about the sales project anyway, there was suddenly a flurry of looks passed among these leaders. "I have let our Director of Training know that I want each of you to partner with a trainer to deliver this session."

I expected some verbal groans or pushback, but there was only the glistening of tiny beads of sweat breaking out on foreheads. Never forget that even for leaders, public speaking is the number one fear. I think some of these leaders imagined leading an eight-hour class because they looked panic-stricken. The room grew silent.

The CEO paused, then said, "I need to know that each of you is committed to this and are willing to train it."

One leader raised his hand and said, "I have one question. Are you talking about just leading one session?"

The CEO smiled. "No, I don't think one session would cover your whole region, do you?"

Mike stepped in and added, "You will have anywhere from six to nine sessions to lead, depending upon the size of your region. Each class will last eight hours. If preparation time is added, this could be a 100 hour commitment."

Groans filled the room. The same regional leader asked, "How do you expect us to lead our region when we'll be out with traveling, maybe eighteen days in one month?"

The CEO responded with a smile. "You will be leading your region, just on the road and in the classroom rather than in an office or a meeting. This is the most important initiative we have right now, so I can't really think of a better way to lead, can you?"

They knew a leader who truly believed in leadership had bested them. Once the CEO completed his announcement, I stepped up and began the training session.

From what I could tell, the CEO was the only one in the room who took notes in his leader's guide. In fact, they had all been given the leader's guide before the session, and the CEO had come to the meeting with yellow post-it notes and questions already written down. That day, the CEO was the most involved participant I ever had in a class full of leaders. Not surprisingly, he would end up leading some of the best training sessions.

My training session with the company leaders was not perfect, nor did I expect it to be. There was one gentleman in particular, Wes, who was the opinion leader of the group and he was particularly disgruntled about the initiative. About an hour into the session, he stood up and said, "You know, I speak for about 70% of the guys in this room when I say I don't like this sales process. I think it's a mistake."

I stood quietly, looking to the CEO to see if he was going to speak. He didn't. I looked to the Head of Retail to see if he would speak. He didn't. This particular regional leader intimidated most of the leaders—he dominated most rooms he entered.

Finally, I responded, "Well, Wes, you all are losing money right now and you have been for a while. I think this change will turn that loss around. If you have a better idea, and I sincerely mean this, share it with us now and we'll go with your idea. But if you don't, then I think we need to try it my way for a while."

Well, Wes didn't have a better idea. Later that night, he approached me and said, "This is my problem, not yours. I'll work it out." I always appreciated his honesty.

Any concern I had about the presentation skills of the company leaders was quickly put to rest once I observed the first sessions they led. The absolute power of having the top dog leading the change overrode any awkward moments of stilted presentation. The trainers did an awesome job of balancing the training facilitation. Fortunately, even when certain company leaders who were a little dry in their delivery, the participants were still mesmerized because they were watching a company leader running the training session. Some of the employees had never even met the head of their region, much less had the chance to interact with him in a class.

I had the honor of partnering with one of the leaders, and I'll never forget our ninth and final session. He stood in front of our last class and talked to his employees about how proud he was of each of them and the work they did every day. He announced this was his last session, and suddenly began to cry. I think it surprised even him. As I looked at those in the room, every eye filled with tears as they witnessed the emotion of a leader who believed in them in a way that came from his heart. And, in that moment, he touched their hearts.

I have never seen sales results lift as quickly as they did with that particular client. Within four weeks, we saw a significant lift in sales that continued at the bank until a merger a couple years later. It was exciting to see a situation where a CEO took his leadership responsibilities seriously, jumped in with both feet, and put his heart and soul into the change plan.

CHANGE LESSON

Leaders Need to Lead

The greatest leaders in the world know that to truly affect change you have to be the person in front. There is a story about General George S. Patton and his second-in-command during World War II trying to figure out where they could best cross a river with the fewest drowning fatalities. After hours of strategic discussion, Patton left the tent. He came back hours later with his uniform dripping wet. He walked over to the map table, pointed to a spot and declared, "We'll cross right here." That's leadership!

If more leaders would step up to the task and ask, "How can I best lead this?" their results would be amazing. And there isn't a report or piece of data that is more important than a leader going out into the population he or she is leading and show a willingness to roll up his or her sleeves and get dirty. Remember: People will follow you, if you are willing to truly lead. 🕉

CHANGE LESSON

True Leadership Inspires

True leaders recognize that most of their employees want to succeed, and they inspire people through their actions. Leadership words are not inspiring if they are not preceded by action. The words might be temporarily motivating, but they don't cause someone to change their mind about a change initiative.

A leader who takes the right action and then says, "Follow me," will get positive results quickly. Leaders who rely on training and communications to generate change when they, themselves, are not willing to lead, will have a tough time inspiring change. It really is that simple: Leadership cannot be delegated. 8

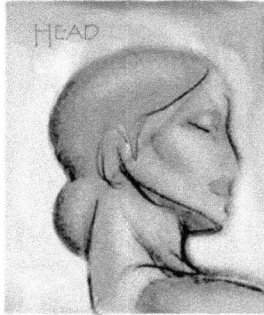

Stay Focused

"The single biggest problem in communication is the illusion that it has taken place."

George Bernard Shaw
Irish Playwright, Author, and Orator

CHAPTER XII

Some Will Follow, Some Will Fall

*T*here are leaders who resist any new change. If they have been at the top of the pyramid in the current work environment, then changing that environment could mean toppling their dominant position. High performance leaders will step up to the task and find a new way to the top, but mediocre leaders who have won via presence in a particular market will fight tooth and nail to keep the status quo. Their number one initiative is protecting their own comfort zone. Understandably, when they are on top, they want to go slow — if they have to go at all! In doing this, they set themselves up as the protector from the demons of change.

Leaders who begin to over protect their employees during times of change feel threatened themselves. Rather than admit their fear of losing position or power, they create an odd super hero. I call these leaders the "Super-Same." Super-Same leaders make sure that nothing will change. To do this, they rally their direct reports under the mantra of "protect our people." They run through their regions, capes flying, saying, "Look at me, I'm your hero!" Well, a true hero doesn't keep his or her employees from moving forward and improving the organization. A true hero finds new ways to save employees rather than ensuring their demise by refusing to change.

I had one such leader with whom I worked in a large corporation. Susan had let me know, in no uncertain terms, that she did not like the change that was coming. After my assessment and recommendation, the company was moving to a performance environment that required people to do things differently in their jobs, and Susan was determined to protect her employees from what she considered an unnecessary evil. I met with Susan several times, and tried to convince her that she was only hurting those who worked for her because their performance would drop while everyone else's would improve. Susan did not listen, and whenever I visited her office to try to explain this to her, she would stand up and walk me to her door, making it clear I was not welcomed.

I knew the way the company's performance results had been measured for the past ten years meant that Susan's market benefited. The positioning of her branches ensured that she always came out on top, regardless of the true skills of her employees. Understandably, Susan liked being the best, and even though most of her success had to do with market position, she easily convinced herself that nobody could beat her results. Susan's fear of this new performance system caused her to be a major speed bump on the road to change — she felt she was in a lose/lose situation. She was a popular leader, and if she fought the change, she would lose support of leadership. On the other hand, if Susan accepted the change plan, her region would no longer be at the top of the rankings.

I tried to appeal to Susan's sense of leadership, letting her know that whatever she did from this point forward would impact those who worked for her. If she supported the change, her employees would be positioned to succeed because they would have the performance skills they needed to compete with the other regions.

Once we completed the change rollout, each region would be reviewed to see if the new performance behaviors were being used and the regions were supporting the new performance process. During a meeting with Susan, I warned her that her region was being positioned to fail, and she had only six months to turn it around. I could sense her fear, and truly wanted to help her move forward any way that I could, but Susan dismissed the entire effort.

Six months later, I worked with regional leaders to conduct the performance review. Out of eight regions, Susan's region ranked last. The saddest part was that her region was already suffering from her stubborn resistance to change. The other regions were flourishing with the change plan, showing increased sales as well as service quality results.

The leaders who experienced the most success did the following:

- Learned as much about the new performance effort as they could so that they could implement it effectively.
- Created a detailed implementation plan, allowing their local leaders to come up with strategies so they could be part of its success.
- Kicked off the change plan with enthusiasm, and stayed enthusiastic during the training sessions.
- Constantly communicated successes and information needed to keep their teams moving forward.
- Tweaked the implementation as needed, based upon what they learned.

Our reluctant leader did the following:

- Resisted the plan immediately, and discounted it as soon as she realized it would negatively impact her rankings.
- Told her direct reports that she would protect them from these "unnecessary changes."
- Stopped communicating any of the information about the performance program.
- Kept doing things the way she had always done them, hoping the change would go away.

After we delivered the results of the review, Susan moved from being obstinate to an obvious state of panic. Suddenly, she realized that this change wasn't going to disappear, but she might. Since I was the messenger, she made her way to my office immediately after I had presented the information. She drilled me on the information I had delivered, trying to shoot holes in the results. When that approach didn't work, she asked me why I was trying to get her fired. During the course of this hour-long conversation, she moved from sarcasm to sincerity, and laughter to anger, not moving forward but stuck in a widening circle.

There were several of those conversations in my office, and I allowed them because I knew, as a change warrior, that she needed a place to vent. Susan's greatest fear was being exposed and she didn't want to admit that maybe, just maybe, she was responsible for her results. After the fourth meeting, I finally told Susan, "I am not responsible for these results, you are, and I will do anything I can to help you move forward at this point."

Eventually, she moved on to another opportunity at another company. Naturally, the real issues went far beyond the review. It is an unfortunate situation, since many times it is a standout leader in the old regime that struggles in the new regime. However, most of the time I have found that those standouts who fail stood out for the wrong reason—ineffective measurement, poor tracking, and senior leadership bias.

Depending on the significance of the change, if there is a leader who refuses to go along with the change, then he or she needs to move on. Not just for the sake of the company, but for the sake of the leader resisting the change. In Susan's case, something had shifted that created an environment in which she was not comfortable. Because she couldn't adjust to the change, she would have been miserable trying to move forward.

Just be prepared, as a change warrior, to shoulder some of the blame. Remind yourself that your role is to move forward with change, not to be loved by all. However, people are still yearning for their comfort zone and are quick to jump to fear at this point in change. In the end, remember that at the same time you are dealing with one angry leader, you have several other leaders who are busy making the change work and leading their regions to greater victory.

CHANGE LESSON

Importance of Alignment

Sometimes people resist change because they believe it is not the right thing to do. Most who resist change for this reason will then suggest other solutions, showing they don't want to stop all movement forward, they just think it could be done more effectively.

However, when leaders resist something that is best for the company simply because they see no way that they are going to win, they have lost their foundation of honor and integrity. They will argue that they are protecting their people, but they are actually acting out of self-interest. Their fear of losing overrides their concern for the company. Alignment is the willingness to move forward for the greater good, even if it means you might suffer. Leaders who are not willing to align are unhealthy influences on every person.

CHANGE LESSON

Some People Need a Way Out

Change warriors tend to think that everybody should be thrilled with change. Well, what if the change creates a job you no longer like? As a change warrior, I have seen some leaders who have had their jobs change significantly due to some new initiative, and they have become miserable as a result. When leaders are miserable, they tend to either go into protective mode with their employees or they withdraw and do as little as possible. Either way, they can potentially undermine the change effort and keep their employees from learning skills to succeed and move forward with the company.

Occasionally, a leader simply needs a way out of the organization because he or she doesn't fit with the new direction. Change can be hard, and there are casualties. Not because they are weaker than other people, but because the change does not fit them.

Most people who leave in these situations ultimately find a sense of relief. They might be angry at first, that is a natural part of the emotional process of change, but eventually they will be grateful. New opportunities await them.

Some work-culture changes result in fairly significant churn. For the majority who stay, the change is reenergizing. Change reinvents the employees just as it reinvents the company.

CHAPTER XIII

Phasing Out Phantoms

*C*haos is good because it is the shortest part of the change process and guarantees that the new reality of change is very close. Chaos is frightening because it contains within it the point at which you must let yourself wallow in the unknown. Imagine you are a trapeze novice, climbing up the ladder for your first swing. Your heart pounds as you climb, finally reaching the small platform and grasping the trapeze in both hands. You jump off the platform, swinging into the air. Chaos is the point at which you let go of one trapeze, still unable to see or grab the next trapeze. You are simply flying through space with no guarantees.

Just as serious change begins, people can swing back to their anger and denial that change is occurring. That is why it is so important for a change warrior to prepare a company's leadership in advance, clearly explaining that the change initiative will cause some fear; and to absolutely get commitments from all the leaders that there will be no going backwards.

Growing up in Southern California, my family lived right at the base of the foothills of the San Bernardino Mountains where we had a clear view of the shape of an arrowhead, created naturally by brush that had been growing on that mountain for thousands of years. We loved the arrowhead that covered most of the side of a mountain, but usually couldn't see it because of smog. The air in California has improved since 1968, but at that time the smog could get so thick your eyes would water and your lungs would feel as if you had smoked ten packs of cigarettes.

Since we often had to stay inside during recess because of poor air quality, we all looked forward to the natural phenomenon known as the Santa Ana winds. Each year these winds blew across the Los Angeles basin for a few days, sometimes reaching up to 70 miles per hour. They were warm desert winds that blew with a fierce determination. One would think this would frighten a child, but I loved to hear these winds that began as whispers and grew to mighty howling. I knew when I awoke in the morning I could see the mountains so clearly it seemed I could trace that arrow with my fingers.

Of course, these winds held a potential dark side that could be highly destructive. If Southern California was in a drought and the environment was dry, there could be fires in the mountains fueled by the winds. Firefighters then faced huge brush fires that could spread in just minutes because of the high winds. Worse, the winds could suddenly change direction, causing the fire to encircle firefighters on the mountainside, forming a disastrous fiery trap. Firefighters tried to stay in constant contact with one another in order to stay in front of the dangerous mix of fire and strong winds. Their persistent communication could mean the difference between life and death.

There were times when my family, along with the neighbors, gathered in the street to watch the fire move down the mountains. We all talked about what *might* happen. Since we didn't have any regular updates (no cell phones, only the six o'clock news report), we tried to figure out what was going on without any substantive information. One neighbor would say, "I heard that there's not enough firemen to fight this fire." Another would chime in, "I hear they've already evacuated the neighborhood just up from us and that we're next."

Most of these stories never panned out, but we spent a lot of time and effort listening to them. As a neighborhood, we created a phantom comprised of "what ifs" because of the lack of communication and our fearful imaginations.

Change is the same way. Sometimes a lack of communication can ignite imaginary phantoms. A company's leadership has been in constant conversation about the change initiative for months before the employees are involved. Leaders have been planning and moving forward, and of course, the employees get the "word on the street" that something is coming down the pike. Exactly what is going on is unclear; the employees don't have the total truth yet because the process isn't complete. Therefore, their imaginations run wild and the rumor mills go into overtime.

One client with whom I worked internally to conduct team building was a leader in his financial services company, but had a reputation for being incredibly sarcastic and condescending to his direct reports. The sales people within this organization did everything possible to avoid interacting with this man, knowing if he gave them a call or paid them a visit it would only pertain to extremely bad news. His numerical results were great, but his interpersonal skills were destructive.

The CEO hired me to meet weekly with this leader. After conducting an assessment, I told him that his team didn't work well together, and a change needed to occur or he was going to lose top leaders. Rather than consider himself a part of the issue, this leader decided to have the training department conduct some team training, relying on the predictable quick fix that diverts attention from the real problem.

I tried to explain to him that training wasn't necessarily the answer to his relationship issues, but he didn't respond. He looked through me as if I had never said anything, using the broken-record technique, repeatedly saying, "I need this training to begin in two weeks." I was not in a position to change his mind, so I worked with the Director of Training to develop the right program.

Weeks later, we began the first team-building session, which included an hour lunch with this leader conversing with his team. For starters, the introduction of the team-building session was awkward since nobody had received the communication I had helped develop explaining why this class was being offered. Instead, the night before class this leader notified his employees that they would be expected to attend the training session. When I asked why it was handled this way, the leader told me he had made the training mandatory and that adults shouldn't have to be coerced into coming to a mandatory training. At that point, I had yet to convince upper management that this leader's relationship skills were the biggest problem. So, I had to trust that these sessions would either provide the proof or a breakthrough.

At lunchtime, this leader walked through the door for his question/answer period, which was supposed to include a lot of communication about the future of the company. While I admired his willingness to do this, the effect he had on the room was negative. The moment he walked in, conversation stopped, people became fascinated by their shoes, and nobody said a word. He gave a brief introduction, but didn't really offer any information. Then he asked if anybody had any questions for him. One brave soul raised her hand and said, "I don't know why we're having this training. Is there something we don't know?"

This leader sarcastically replied, "If there was, then I'd say there's a reason why you don't know it." That kind of response from this leader was the antithesis of these "team building" sessions.

After he walked out, the people in the room began talking again. I heard comments like, "We're toast. He's just not saying that we're going to be downsized." One woman began texting other colleagues as quickly as possible, since they were the first of more than 120 people who would have this training. I told everybody to put down their phones and then tried to diffuse the phantom this irresponsible leader had created. Because I was aware of the CEO's requirement, I knew that the only reason for the training sessions was because the CEO had told this difficult leader to build better team relationships and the leader felt this was the first step.

Even when I told this group that the training was simply part of a new effort to build better teamwork, they didn't believe it. The determination of that leader to hold his cards close to the vest as a form of intimidation created emotional chaos. Rumors flew, people looked for other jobs, and top performers walked out the door. A few months later, the CEO asked this leader to resign, but the damage was done. His lack of communication left a void, and that void was filled with a phantom created by fear and speculation.

When a phantom rears its troublesome head in the midst of a change initiative, a change warrior must be prepared to sound an alert that it is time to beef up timely communication. Some of those warning phrases to watch out for include:

- Did you hear that...?
- I heard that....
- Do you know what my manager said . . .?

Those types of phrases among employees create chaos because they whip up rumors while leaders are sitting in meetings looking at project plans. What leadership fails to realize is that while they are busy constructing their complicated project plans, they are losing the employees' trust. Hypothetical rumors can influence employees to quit, and guess who leaves first? Unfortunately, it is usually the top achievers who are most likely to get job offers at other companies. Never underestimate the power of imagination and stories to create phantoms. People will believe the phantoms because they have no other messages of truth with which to replace them. The phantoms become their reality.

The good news is that communication can make a challenging change initiative run remarkably more smoothly. Communication is like putting the best synthetic oil in your car. While the car might not do anything remarkable, the drive is suddenly without chugs and coughs. By planning a communication strategy first, change warriors can prevent months of handling employee loss and fear.

I worked with one mid-sized bank that offered over one hundred different types of checking and savings accounts.

They were simplifying their deposit products from one hundred to five. This would inconvenience more than 35% of current bank customers, and there was a concern that the customers impacted by the change would leave their bank branches and migrate to local community banks. We arranged a series of communications that included several different parts:

- Clearly written communication to the customers about the improvement in bank deposit products.
- Scripts for bank employees who would make follow-up phone calls to customers.
- Scripts for employees to handle any customer objections to those phone calls.
- Communications for bank leaders from the top down, focusing on the benefits to those who reported directly to the leaders.
- Communications for bank leaders addressing the possible objections they might receive from employees and how to respond to those objections. We also provided responses to any additional questions employees might ask.

As a result of these changes, that bank lost less than 1% of its customers during that change initiative because everybody knew what to expect and how to handle it. Change warriors must encourage leadership to keep employees informed throughout every phase of the change, even when things seem to be running smoothly. Every stage of change requires constant communication. If a company's leaders and employees can make it through chaos, their new reality is just around the corner.

CHANGE LESSON

Communication Is Number One

Sometimes leadership is six months to a year ahead of their employees regarding change initiatives. Company leaders forget about this time lag between realities, and tend to assume that once they have kicked off the change initiative, they can go back to planning and let the change take care of itself.

Great change warriors know they have to keep reminding leaders to communicate with their employees. Change warriors realize employees are still fearful when a change initiative takes hold company wide because the employees do not really know where the change is going to end and how it will ultimately affect them. Whenever things get quiet, employees assume the worst. Their "truth" ceases to be shaped by leadership, and instead, the rumor mill takes over. This results in a distorted view of the truth that can cause the loss of top employees.

Communication must be three things — clear, consistent, and honest. You cannot over communicate during times of change. Communication cannot slow down or stop at any stage of change. If employees cannot be told the truth about impending change, then the company leaders need to review the entire change process. To build employee trust in the process, the truth must be told consistently throughout every phase of change.

CHANGE LESSON

Chaos Is a Good Sign

Chaos is a terrifying point when making tough changes, but a necessary one. It is also a sign that you are close to the end of the change journey.

Change is not comfortable or predictable, and there will be tough times when everyone must continue to make the change one step at a time—even when things go dark. However, as a wise firefighter once responded to my laments about the destructive force of those fires in the San Bernardino Mountains, "Fires also clear out brush and debris, creating extremely fertile soil. It serves a purpose."

Change warriors know that chaos clears out the brush of unnecessary past change initiatives. At the same time, leaders must constantly communicate with their employees, especially during chaotic times. The danger of the chaos phase is that people can choose to return to a place of denial, or worse, they can bail out of the effort altogether. Leaders must step up at this point, tell the truth, and have confidence that people can handle more than they think they can.

People are willing to let go of their comfort zone if they know the journey ahead has a noble purpose and a confident leader.

SECTION SIX

Recognize a New Reality

---

*"Culture does not change because we desire
to change it. Culture changes when the
organization is transformed; the culture
reflects the realities of people
working together every day. "*

Frances Hesselbein
Former National Director of Girl Scouts

CHAPTER XIV

From Chaos to Cooperation

*C*hange warriors know that if leaders can get through the stages of fear and chaos, the change effort is almost complete. In his book, *Managing at the Speed of Change*, Daryl Connor shares his premise that people will choose the familiarity of the known over the anxiety of the unknown. His change model asserts that people impacted by change begin with uninformed optimism, move to informed pessimism, and then eventually find their way to hopeful realism. Change leaders have to understand that unless they are willing to weather the change, they will never experience the rainbow at the end.

Shortcuts to change rarely provide stunning new realities. You find the best results at the end of the change journey when people pull together. One company I worked with was trying to move into a business culture that provided the proper technology to support salespeople. Previously, it had been a staff-focused company, and the salespeople seemed to be a necessary evil. A part of the change was for leadership to remind staff that the revenue generated by salespeople made their jobs possible. Once staff rediscovered this fundamental aspect of a successful business, they had a new love and concern for their salespeople.

This company hired me to help its leaders come together to create a customer-focused sales process that satisfied both the staff and the sales teams. I spent fourteen months with the company leaders rolling out town-hall meetings for employees and ensuring that sales trainers taught the necessary sales skills to every employee. We also created a company-wide sales language and sales approach that every line of business in the company used. This meant we had to eliminate several other sales programs and consultants. Several company leaders were not happy with this streamlining and I faced intense moments of unpopularity, but the company employees in all the various divisions started to click with the changes.

What had been a constant battle between lines of business for everything from types of training to human resource policies to technology, was now becoming a journey of fellow travelers. Under the new sales initiative, the company behaviors were beginning to be as universal as our sales language, and positive results made all the company employees believers. We were leaving the chaos behind and moving into a new reality with a changed company culture.

In one particularly amazing technology session, all the divisions of this company gelled and became one cohesive unit. In the previous fourteen months, we had all worked together to develop the sales and service behaviors that would develop a great experience for the company's customers. Now, we needed the technology to back it up since every division of the company wanted a new contact management system. We knew the time was right because the change leaders already had the employees' change behaviors in place. (Too many companies make the mistake of wanting the contact management system first. People sell, not systems.)

Change warriors know that while customer relationship tools can be extremely helpful, they do not miraculously increase sales. It is like someone who dreams of writing that great novel but waits to get the best laptop before they begin writing. If they won't write that novel on a legal pad, then they're not going to write it on a laptop.

We were proud of the fact that we made the behavior journey first. We had spent almost two years determining which behaviors created the kind of sales and service environment we wanted for our customers. Now, we were going to create the technology to support it.

We started by listing every division in the company that impacted sales reporting and behaviors, and asked each division leader to send one representative to a two-day brainstorming session. In addition, we brought in a new technology leader who was building a strong team. If the company was going to build a homegrown system, it was going to be the best—not something held together with rubber bands and paper clips.

More than fifty people representing all the divisions of the company attended the brainstorming session, and all were ready to create something new. People chose to sit at tables with colleagues from other departments they didn't know well, creating a sense of camaraderie and optimism. The festive energy in the room was incredibly positive. I could sense the powerful presence of hopeful realism. People were filled with the courage of a group that had survived changes during the past year and felt they had made a difference in the company. They were starting to be comfortable with the changes they had helped implement.

The brainstorming session began by introducing a new internal customer relationship management system. We also introduced the gentleman who would be the new leader of technology. The group welcomed him with warm applause— something that would not have occurred fourteen months earlier when we first began the change initiative. Rather than appearing to be a potential threat, the group saw the new technology leader as someone who had the knowledge to create the right technology to move the company forward. Now, company leadership focused on improvement rather than protection.

The objective of the session had to be determined first, so we asked the large group: Why is it important that we have a contact management system?

They all agreed that the system would be about two benefits:

- To better serve our external customers.
- To help employees do their job more effectively.

I was thrilled the company representatives addressed both the customer and the employee needs, understanding that if either was not properly served, the entire effort would be a waste of time. To keep us focused during the meeting, we posted the words on the wall, "CUSTOMER" and "EMPLOYEE," to remind us of what was truly important.

Then, we broke the group into teams with similar business concerns so the different areas within the company could identify what they needed a contact management system to offer. We had ten teams, including a human resources team, an investment team, a mortgage team, and a retail team. We asked each team to answer the following question:

- *If we could have the perfect contact management system, what would it include?*

After twenty minutes of brainstorming, each group was asked to review its ideas and determine if any were *not* focused on the customer's experience. If so, they were to delete those ideas. Then, they reviewed their ideas to make sure they would actually make an employee's life easier, and removed any that would not. Finally, each group selected a spokesperson who shared the team's specific ideas. We knew this group felt they were given a platform to voice their opinions and we were listening. The suggestions were focused and creative. Nobody seemed to be "stumping" for his or her area; instead, everyone was truly working together for the greater good.

Next, we divided everyone into diverse groups, and asked them to develop a plan that would meet everyone's needs while complementing others. Once those lists were completed, we brought the group together, listing all the elements of the internal system developed by each team. Once we had all of the elements listed, we took the following actions:

- Combined similar elements.
- Deleted elements that would not be possible with current capabilities.
- Ranked according to importance the elements we felt would be foundational and should be created first.

The ranking allowed us to develop the next steps that were realistic and doable. So often it seems that corporate initiatives are stalled because there is no incremental approach to the steps that need to be taken first. Everybody seems to think you have to do it all or do nothing at all. Usually, nothing at all is the result.

There was a lot of hard work during this two-day meeting. Amazingly, people were willing to let go of certain system elements if it made everything easier for the customer and the employee. For anybody in the corporate environment, you can understand what a miracle this moment represented. At the end of two days, we had put together a "dream system" that our technology director would work to implement. Over the next six months his team worked to build the system.

To keep communication flowing during the technological development, we did the following:

- Made sure the original team was kept in the loop, both on what was working and what was not.
- Used team members as points of contact for any problem-solving that was needed.
- Provided communication tools to leadership so that all employees would be clear about the new offerings and be as informed as anyone on the team.
- Worked our sales and service behaviors into every communication to keep the company-wide language active.
- Made sure every line of business within the company understood how the new components would drive business to them.

Each quarter we introduced a couple of new components, giving employees the time to learn how to use just a couple of new steps on the system without stumbling in front of the customer. More importantly, each of the components was on the original "wish list" of the different company departments. Our internal contact management system included a profile that was tied to follow-up calls and incentive plans. Rankings were available to show how each store was competing, and we provided coaching plans for improving rankings with specific behaviors. Our sales checklists were also made available, and were tied into the conversational elements of the system.

The most amazing part of that entire effort was the fact that a team that had been struggling through change came together with ease and worked hard to progress. Together, the employees grabbed the tools we could bring to the table and used them to build a system that offered something for everybody while staying focused on the customer.

We had come through the chaos of change, and now, the company was moving toward a new reality. Suddenly, the new way of doing things became the employees' expectation. As a team of change warriors, we had digested the change and we were lean and mean and feeling really good about the work we had done.

CHANGE LESSON

Energy of Change

Change warriors recognize when employees are willing to work together on a project this means the dark days of company-infighting are fading away. When people emerge from chaos, there is an energy that is palpable as everyone realizes they made it through the tough part of change and they survived it. The challenging part of moving from chaos into a new work reality is that you have to be willing to sit in the chaos for a while when every part of you wants to go back to your comfort zone. You have to trust that the breakthrough to a new reality is close at hand.

Breakthrough most often reveals itself through an increase in collaboration. When teams let go of their silo-mentality, they can focus on problem-solving rather than protecting turf. When they join forces, the light of progression begins to shine.

CHANGE LESSON

The New Comfort Zone

Sometimes, we assume change must be incredibly dramatic and new. Change warriors know that real change evolves in incremental steps. Small steps prevent change paralysis. Before people realize it, they have made change a part of their every day life. Once the change is established, it becomes the new comfort zone.

When employees believe the change will be beneficial, will stick, and is doable, they incorporate it into every day life. After the change becomes a part of every day behaviors, it becomes known and comfortable, and ceases to be change.

Change warriors are courageous leaders who are motivated by the unknown. Once change has converted to the comfort zone, it is time for the change warrior to move on to the next challenge.

CHAPTER XV

When to Wave Good-bye

*S*ometimes, the most difficult part of being a change warrior is knowing when to leave. After weathering the storms and journeying up the mountain to create a new company reality, you would like to enjoy the view for a while. But you probably shouldn't, because change warriors have a tendency to chip away at their own work if they stay around. After all, change warriors are about change and rather than being content to coast on calm waters, we might tend to stir up an unnecessary storm.

Change warriors always need to pass the baton to those who will sustain the change. Never create an environment where leaders must lean on you long after the change has been completed. While it is tempting as an employee who stepped up to be a change warrior to stay in the temporary change role you have helped create — don't.

For change warriors hired from the outside, I understand you might be tempted by continued income, but don't stay. Letting go of the change warrior role proves that you are truly a great leader. Change warriors leave people stronger and more capable of handling change than when they met them.

And once an effort has moved to its point of being the new reality, it is time to move to the next change challenge.

When moving on, a change warrior can experience deep emotions. I had experienced a particularly stressful change effort with one financial group when I was an internal employee serving in the position of change leader. I had worked to implement a new program that had caused the CEO to fire several leaders. For a few months after that, I felt fiercely unpopular. The feeling was confirmed when an employee who worked for one of the fired leaders actually left a death threat on my desk. The note referenced where I parked, and the person who threatened me had taken my photos of my kids off my desk. Needless to say, I had escorts to my car. The company finally identified the angry person and had him removed from his job. It was a harrowing few months.

This was the only time in my career as a change warrior that I was threatened with physical harm, and I am glad it was the only time. I spent a lot of time reviewing the situation, examining if I had really done something that deserved such a response. In the meantime, other leaders were frustrated with the new process we were introducing, and I ate a lot of lunches by myself. However, I hung in there because I knew the change was right, and there were other leaders who had linked arms with me.

My job during those unpopular months was to keep my eye on the prize and build relationships with leaders and show the value of the change. I traveled to different regions and put in extra training and observation hours. The regions began to see success, and the ice melted around my relationships with employees who had kept me at arm's length. Being an internal change warrior can be particularly challenging, since you must sit in the environment where colleagues are unhappy and listen to their frustrations every day. I did, and found some of my greatest relationships in those conversations.

Less than a year later, the change was complete. Everybody's region was running more smoothly because of the behaviors we had implemented, and we had all bonded by meeting the challenges and coming out on the side of the new reality. At a meeting with my manager, I announced it was time for me to move on. I knew this change was complete, and another area of the bank had a new change opportunity that needed my help. My manager was flabbergasted when I told him I was leaving, and he said to me, "Why would you leave this position now? You created it, and you're at the mountaintop."

I thought about it and replied, "I don't like sitting on the mountain top; I like the climb that got me there."

Instead, I decided to accept the chance to climb another mountain, and now I had to tell the team that had made the previous climb with me that I was leaving. I will never forget that day. In our final meeting, each one of the leaders voluntarily shared how it had been working together around change and how how much they valued the relationships forged. I looked around the room and realized that while change is sometimes painful, if it is the right change, it is always worth the pain. By the end of the meeting, we were all fighting tears, sometimes not so successfully.

When the retail leader handed me a gift with tears in his eyes, I doubted my decision for a moment. I asked myself, *Why would I leave this environment I'd worked so hard to help create?* I revisited the reasons for my decision. Change warriors need to understand the signs that let you know it is time to move on. Some of them include:

- Leaders begin to do some of the things you have been doing, and they don't need your help.
- People talk the same language around the initiative.
- There is new energy, and people are problem solving.
- Growth is occurring, reflected in behavioral and numerical results.
- People ask to do some of what you have been doing in the past, and they are capable of doing it.
- The CEO and company leaders are on board.
- Change has become the new comfort zone.

There is a certain courage change warriors must exercise or it will be lost. I had a leader once tell me, "You have the heart of a lion." I savor the opportunities when I can use my own courage. If I don't have a challenge, I will create one. In one of my all-time favorite movies, *The Wizard of Oz*, the cowardly lion finds the great change he was seeking—courage. His response in the movie is like a mantra for me in my work as a change warrior. He says, "Read what my medal says: 'Courage.' Ain't it the truth? Ain't it the truth?"

In addition, change warriors generally are awful at maintenance, once the change initiative is in place. Routine is not a natural state for change warriors. Besides, those who are phenomenal managers are best served if we move on.

Be warned that company leaders will often cling to you with the desperation of a freshman in college clinging to parents as they stand in front of his dorm, trying to say good-bye. This scenario in a business setting looks like company leaders who are sure they can lead the change effort now, but they want you around just in case. You will feel like a parent, wanting to stay around to catch them if they fall. Even worse, your ego will be so enticed by the request to stay that you will be tempted. Warning: Don't become the victim of their fear or your ego.

A year or two down the road, the same company leaders will realize you haven't been necessary for a while and if you are an external, they will resent the money they have paid you. Or else, the leaders will move you from strategic expert to a "pair of hands" knocking out small tasks that are miles from the challenges that drive you.

Change warriors who are internal leaders might not have the opportunity to leave their positions, but once change becomes a successful new reality, they must be ready to take on the next challenge. No matter how badly they might want to stay in the glory of successful change, they cannot. Trying to stay in the realm of a new reality is like expecting the spectacular beauty of fall leaves to stay in place more than a few weeks. New realities, if arrived at correctly, only last a brief period before they turn into a new comfort zone. Once they are in a comfort zone, the change cycle is complete. Hopefully, a leader will have some time to catch his or her breath before the next change, but in today's frantic world it is doubtful. Leaders must keep marching forward.

The true beauty of change is not in the change itself, but in the relationships formed during it. When a change warrior finds other courageous souls, there are moments of magic that go beyond a corporate initiative. Hearts are melded together during the toughest times of battle, and the good-bye—even if simply to this particular initiative—means unlinking arms and joining a new team with a new challenge. The best change warrior leaves a company stronger and the leaders more capable.

In a nutshell, here is what I have learned over twenty years of leading change: A change warrior must have the ability to motivate those involved in change to move forward, the courage to stay with change until it is completed, and the strength to wave good-bye.

CHANGE LESSON

Time to Move On

When change finally reaches the exciting point of a new reality, it is almost over. A new reality in a work culture means the tough part is over, and change is now exciting and people are engaged. The change you have been leading and struggling to achieve will no longer be change, but rather the new reality

Although the new reality is a warm, exciting place to be, a change warrior knows it is not a place to land and stay. Those who have sacrificed to achieve the change might want to set up camp for a while, but it doesn't work. The exciting new place will quickly become the norm, and another storm of change will already be brewing off in the distance.

Change warriors must know when to say good-bye. Once change is almost complete, a change warrior needs to begin to pack his or her bags and get ready to move on. Even internal leaders must understand when it is time to move on to the next challenge. The hard part is letting go

---

because you can form deep bonds with those who have helped make the change succeed. And if you have been an external consultant, company management may offer you a longer working relationship, which can also be enticing.

Whatever the case may be, change warriors must know when it is time to pass the baton. If they don't, most sabotage their own efforts by continuing to create storms of change that wipe out what has already been accomplished. Understand, if you stay around too long, you will continue to create unneeded energy that will confuse a situation rather than complete it. I have told many company leaders, "Once I'm done, let me leave. If I don't, I will keep revisiting this effort because it's what I do."

The greatest change warriors know when to say good-bye. So, I hope you enjoyed my stories and learned from my experiences, but now it is time for me to let go of this book and say good-bye.

Thank you for making this journey with me, and I hope many of you will contact me in the future so we can get to know each other. Until then, I will tap my ruby slippers together three times, and move on.

Good luck to each of you. Now, repeat after me:

> There's no place like change,
> There's no place like change,
> There's no place like change.

About the Author

*D*onna Highfill is the founder and president of Highfill Performance Group (HPG), a dynamic consultancy that prides itself on leading businesses through change initiatives with a focus on moving the

Donna Highfill

TODD BURROW

hearts and minds of the people involved. Donna launched HPG in 2001 after years of increasingly responsible assignments with several top-tier financial services organizations. Her passion has always been helping leaders change the story of their organization through simple, daily actions that lead to improved performance.

Donna has worked with a series of major Fortune 500 financial services institutions as a change strategy and performance consultant, helping them develop leadership teams and sales strategies. She also provides one-on-one coaching for executives with a focus on helping business leaders understand the people side of change.

Donna has written numerous articles on business change that have been published nationally. She co-authored an article,

"The Dark Side of Change," which McGraw Hill included in its anthology of the "most intriguing business articles" for 2005.

Currently, Donna is the author of two blogs;

- a change management blog on her website, www.highfillperformancegroup.com,
- and a blog on her web site for baby-boomer women, www.damenationblog.com.

This is Donna's first book. She lives in Richmond, Virginia with her husband and their two children.

Notes

Notes

Notes

www.ingramcontent.com/pod-product-compliance
Lightning Source LLC
Chambersburg PA
CBHW072347200326
41519CB00015B/3689